WITHDRAWN
UTSA LIBRARIES

A CHURCH WITHOUT GOD

ERNEST HARRISON

A CHURCH WITHOUT GOD

J. B. LIPPINCOTT COMPANY

PHILADELPHIA & NEW YORK

1967

Copyright © 1966 by Ernest Harrison

ALL RIGHTS RESERVED.

No part of this book may be reproduced
in any form without permission in writing
from the publishers, except by a reviewer,
who may quote brief passages in a review
to be printed in a magazine or newspaper.

Grateful acknowledgement is made to the University
of Minnesota Press for permission to quote extracts
from: Leon Festinger, Henry W. Riecken, Jr., and
Stanley Schachter, *When Prophecy Fails,* University of
Minnesota Press, Minneapolis. © Copyright 1956 by
the University of Minnesota.

Library of Congress Catalog Card No.: 67-20437

Printed in the United States of America

Contents

Preface

The original title of this book was *Mother Church Is Dead and Gone — What do the Children do Now?* Though unsuitable, it summarized the theme with some accuracy. Mother Church is no longer a central character in the Christian drama, but the Church remains so. With the collapse of its authoritarian structure, many members are seeking new guidelines to replace those which have hitherto been provided only under "lawful authority." This book offers a few suggestions as to where those guidelines are being found.

In the highly creative and fluid situation which belongs to our day, it would be premature to seek any theological system. The following pages simply attempt to describe, as accurately and honestly as I can, some of the patterns of Christianity which I perceive in the present and which I think the future holds. An increasing number of Christians — to a greater or lesser degree — no longer accept the traditional creeds, doctrines, liturgies, or moral precepts. Yet they consider themselves Christians and hope to be so received; they consider themselves loyal members of their respective denominations and hope to be so received. If this book enables them to feel more confident in their hope — or if it enables those of a more traditional bent to welcome them — then it will be justified.

ERNEST HARRISON

Acknowledgments

In addition to the acknowledgments made in the text, I should like to thank James Fisk and other members of the Holy Trinity congregation, together with Philip Jefferson and the staff of the General Board of Religious Education at Church House, for triggering so many of the ideas in this book; Margot Lods for invaluable criticism of the manuscript; Jane Martin for assistance in the final stages of preparation; Gordon Byce for suggesting the basic research for Chapter V; and, above all, my wife and family for providing the necessary morale and coffee when needed. None of the above is in any way committed to the opinions expressed in the following pages, though I hope they like some of them.

CHAPTER I

The New Freedom

I

This is a book about the Church.

To a first-hand observer, the Church is people speaking, thinking, and acting. There is much talk of God, but God himself does not speak; it is men whose tongues wag, and men whose ear-drums vibrate in response. It is men who think the thoughts that make the tongues wag and men who think the thoughts triggered by the vibrations of their ear-drums. There is much talk of God's work, but God does not work; it is men who lift heavy stones, pound the wood of pulpits, wriggle their knees, bury their noses in books, inject serum into veins, and attend to the sick, the maimed, and the outcast. There is great talk of money for God's work; but it is men who put their hands into their pockets to extract the money they have earned in human activity and in the service of human beings. The money is taken from them by other human beings who use it to pay bills and salaries, to invest in dividend-paying commercial transactions.

This clear fact is implied in such descriptions of the Church as "the People of God" or "the Body of Christ." The emphasis is on people. So the first description of the Church is the only one that finally satisfies: it is the people of God – all of them, whoever they are, in whatever condition, of whatever intellect, whatever emotional stability. If God talks, he talks to them all. If he is silent, or cannot talk, then *none* hears.

If this description of the Church were taken seriously, there would be fewer problems today; and this book would not be necessary. For it is immediately evident that men differ in their interpretations of words like "God" and "Jesus Christ," "Christian" and "Good," "Love" and "Holiness." When given freedom, they take widely different attitudes to any matter which is raised as part of the Church's teaching and practice. The deduction is simple. If it is through the Church that God works, and if the Church is his people, then in order to discover God's will, we have to listen to what people say and think. When we do this, it becomes clear that God is much varied and many-splendoured, that he holds untold and apparently inconsistent forces and ideas within himself and passes them along, with little system or consistency, to his varied and many-splendoured children. He is not particularly logical and makes no effort to be fair; he is no lover of uniformity and shows little anxiety for unity; he makes no two things alike, not two human beings, no two thoughts, no two emotions.

Within this haphazard, bewildering, and beautiful mish-mash,* we sense that all men share much in common. It is not easy to identify this common element except at the physical level – and even here the subtle absence of any predictable law is daily perceived – but it cannot be evaded. There may be no agreement about the after-life or the truth of the Bible, but there is universal recognition of the need for love in all human relationships. The description of God as love needs no wide-ranging philosophical analysis. It is recognized immediately as realistic.

If the Church were seriously accepted as "the People of God," then all their feelings, reactions, and thoughts would be represented in its teaching. But this has not happened. Instead, the people have, either willingly or under duress, passed their right to make decisions into the care of smaller groups. These groups, having taken the initiative and claiming to speak for the rest, come to like the high status that flows from their leadership. They seek to maintain it not only for themselves but for their children,

---

*Well brought out in the National Film Board's movie *Free Fall*, which portrays, in an exciting and impressionistic fashion, the fantastic mixed-up realities of the natural order, including man and his creations.

and for those who can receive the inheritance as children.* So, in the course of time, the Church comes to mean not the people of God but a small coterie which finds the means to impose its will on the rest. Its claims are great and its practices ingenious. Claiming to speak for God, it elevates the simple responses of love into such a complex web of subtle thought that only the occasional rebel can raise questions.

A good example of this process in practice is to be found in the Creeds. These statements of faith are said to be the teachings of "The Church." A simple test made among modern Church people shows that this is far from true. Almost every point raised in the Creeds is doubted by vast numbers of Christians; some are strongly denied. Some, like the Virgin Birth, are received in a lukewarm fashion by the majority of members. Yet they are still announced as doctrines of the Church. The Church, so described, is clearly not the whole people, nor even a majority of them, but a small group that is supposed to know best. When, in the light of Church opinion, some critics have questioned the need to accept the Creeds, the reply usually made is that the doctrines enshrined there can never be changed, because the beliefs set down were revealed by God to the United Church of the first Ecumenical and Undivided Councils.

This restricts the meaning of "The Church" even further. It is now not even a group of powerful people, but a group of such people assembled at one or two points in history. A small Church indeed. And who was assembled? The people of God? How many laymen were present? How many women? How many representatives of the poor or the working classes? How many of the decisions were made by aristocrats and well-educated scholars? How many by men in positions of rapidly increasing power over the lives of others? Does God prefer to speak through scholars, aristocrats, and powerful men? Does he ignore women and the poor?

The chilling fact is that the Creeds represent the view of a mere handful of human beings who tussled with some difficult problems and came up with some answers. That these answers

---

*As, for example, in ordination, when the new priest receives the family legacy and the new bishop the control of it.

were relevant in their day and for many centuries afterwards is attested by the fact that they were accepted, until recently, by most theologians and Church-attenders. Even here, however, we may have good reason to pause. Was the agreement a free response of the people to the truths that were stated, or was some duress used, so that they really had no alternative? Throughout the ages, there were always those who raised voices of protest. The Creeds were maintained in a position of authority against these protests, partly by sound argument, but also by brutal treatment handed out to those who could command neither money, armies, nor the control of the law courts. It is not difficult to believe in a Creed when doing so keeps you in a job and out of prison.

Today it is no longer possible to punish any but the person who wishes to be punished; and only arguments and sincere convictions are available to hold the Christian faithful to the Creeds. The arguments, however, no longer commend themselves; sincere convictions are seen as the prerogative of all men. The Creeds are, as they always were, the declared doctrine, not of the Church as the people of God, but as a coterie of men who claim to enunciate the doctrine, practices, and worship of the Church, together with those others who accept their right to do so. It is a coterie which, even in the twentieth century, retains in its hands most of the money and legal privileges of the Church – but little more.

In this context, it is obvious who Mother Church is. She symbolizes the Church in the narrow sense, the Church which knows what is best for others, and is willing to impose it in the strongest way that society permits. She holds, as I have said, most of the money and the legal privileges delivered from the past; but these are a hollow possession. For the hand, though it grips hard and continues to be heavy, is lifeless.

II

At what point in our history Mother Church died is impossible to say; but its reality is now at last inescapable. She has had a great and awe-inspiring record. She gave most people in the

Western World their birth and took full advantage of the fact. She offered herself as an agent, more precisely, *the* agent of God. She saw her duty to be that of imposing his rules upon her children, disciplining and punishing them, praising and rewarding them, smothering them with affection and smacking their bottoms, screaming at them in rage, demanding their obedience and their constant expressions of loyalty and affection. She destroyed any love they showed for mothers of other families; she gave them security, work to do, frustrations to overcome. She filled them skilfully with guilt upon guilt, so that they would never feel free to escape her apron strings. In the final event, she ate them.

All this she did in the name of God, though the children rarely, if ever, saw him. From time to time, she would beam with especial good will upon a few chosen children who would go apart and return to say that they had seen God and knew what he wanted for the rest. He was, they declared, very grand and could be seen only with the eyes of faith. He lived in a remote place, yet he also moved among them, keeping his fatherly and watchful eye upon them, unseen yet ever present, to be loved and, as Mother Church quite properly insisted, feared.

He administered punishments directly, through the sufferings of the children. This, Mother Church said, was a sign of his love and goodness because there is a depth of merit in pain dutifully borne, and the great creations of men come through sacrifice and misery. If the children complained, as some of them did, that this seemed a strange way to show affection, they were ordered not to be sinful. If they asserted that they felt themselves to be good rather than sinful, they were informed that this could not be so, that they must have evil thoughts, actions, and motives hidden from the sight of others. If they insisted that they could not accept her accusations, Mother Church told them not to be impertinent and cudgelled them into silence with the grandeur of Creation and its uncontrollable natural greatnesses.

Some of God's punishments were administered by Mother Church herself. Because she knew exactly what he wanted, she could do so with great assurance. At times her rage towards disobedient children became paranoiac. She would dash them to pieces, torture them, and send them screaming from her pres-

5

ence. On these occasions, it was not possible to pacify her nor demonstrate her errors, for she claimed that she could not err. When challenged that the tormenting of her children could not be reconciled with her claim to be carrying out the law of a God who was pure and eternal love, she insisted that she worked a deeper love than they knew. Can this, screamed the children whose limbs were torn apart, be a sign of love? Mother Church continued unwrinkled by doubt. Indeed, and was it not for their own sakes that she was forced to punish them? Through suffering, they would finally meet their God and at last please him. And if, at the moment of death, they would confess that they had erred, and that Mother had been right all the time, then all might still be well. In the next world, when they saw the final Truth, they would give her thanks.

Not that it would be easy in the next world. For love must not be mushy or sentimental. God, she explained, did not share this worldly nonsense that love accepts others unconditionally as they are. So, even beyond death, love could only be granted to the deserving, and there would be even more hurt and flames. For those who did not understand, or refused to obey, the flames would never cease; the love of God would be fed by unending torment. Nor could the dying children take from death the comfort that at least they would be free of Mother Church. When God punished her children in Purgatory, she would be right there, still expecting.

This, however, was only one side of Mother Church. If you obeyed her, agreed with everything she did, ran her errands dutifully, worked hard for her, spoke kindly of her to other families and outsiders, fought and killed those who opposed her, then her smile was benign. She offered exaltation and security, gave life and health, and beamed with a gay abandon upon her faithful children. Her own sex life must have been disappointing, for she was clearly embarrassed by signs of it in her children; but, provided they took care to be reticent and meet each other under strict life-long regulations, she was willing to bless even this.

Nor did she always set a price-tag on her blessings. She loved even those distant families who did not know her. She built hospitals for them and sent her children to staff them. She built schools and sent her children to teach in them. She erected mental homes and crèches for the care of the fallen. Above all, she raised great temples in which to worship the God whom the privileged among her children had been permitted to see. To those who performed their tasks well, she gave great rewards; and herself became fat.

Now, towards the end of the twentieth century, she is dead. Nobody knows when she died, and there is yet to be a public burial. There are, indeed, some who insist that she is still here, and they speak constantly of her with loud and insistent pride. But the acts of her strength, which they praise, though they are occasionally in the present, fall mostly in the past, in the great days of old. The obedience to her will, which was so marked when the echo of her laugh and the crack of her whip could be heard in all lands, is no longer seen. Even those of her children who say that she is still alive attend her great temples only when the whim possesses them, and the faithful may be deterred from doing so by the most trivial of events; unless their desires are clearly and palpably met, they will withhold the money that is needed to staff her hospitals, schools, and temples.*

Some of those who insist that she still lives talk realistically and are fully aware of the normal life of ordinary men. They admit openly that she is ill, but they declare that she is receiving strong doses of sound medicine and that, under the skilful care of her new-style doctors, she will recover. Some go so far as to report that she is a changed woman. Those of her children who talk in this way of her recovery do so with great vitality, so much so that the less courageous free-thinkers who believe her to be dead occasionally hesitate. They move cautiously. Recalling the objects she admired in her hey-day, they ensure that there are still some schools and hospitals dedicated to her glory; they continue to call upon her God to bless her national enterprises. If the rumour that she is still alive proves to be right, then, when she returns to power, she will be pleased to see that they were not disobedient in all things.

---

*A bishop has assured me three times that several clergy have reported to him that the financial giving in their Churches has dropped largely because of the publication of Pierre Berton's *The Comfortable Pew*.

But the days pass, she does not appear, and the conclusion can no longer be resisted. She is dead and will never return to life. There is some sadness in this, for the great achievements of her prime are built into our Western way of life. Were it not for her, we might have no schools, hospitals, literature, or works of charity. Yet she is no longer needed for any of these. We can have good schools without her, good hospitals, good literature, and good works of charity. We can, in fact, have better – and will continue to have still better – as we learn to accept the fact of her death. For, in her anxiety about herself, she put too high a price on so many of her gifts. Though she inspired medicine, she also held it back; though she was the harbinger of education, she denied it freedom; though she encouraged literature, music, and art, she also censored them; though she cared for the poor, she taught them not to rebel; though she instructed masters to respect their slaves, she approved too long their respective ranks. She thought always in terms of hierarchy, the giving and obeying of orders. Though she spoke for all men, she ate too often at the tables of the rich.

III

Already her death has brought freedom to many of her children. The coterie of people, mostly men, whose decision-making power she symbolizes, no longer imposes its will; and it is no surprise to find that, as the power of the institutional Church crumbles, we find among Christians more freedom of thought, speech, and writing than among any other group in our society. The freedom is not complete, nor is it accepted without grudge, but it is there. Other institutions, whether strong or weak, concede no freedom at all. If an executive of United Steel, International Chemical Industries, or Lever Brothers publicly lists some of his firm's shortcomings, the truth of his statements provides no protection; he will be fired. If a high employee of General Motors, Ford, or Chrysler admits that his firm's automobiles are unsafe, the truth of his charge will not help him; he will find himself without work. If an employee of a large department store refuses to accept a promotion, which requires that he sack another employee of long standing, his honesty will avail him nothing; he will be shown neither mercy nor pity. Nor is the denial of freedom limited to the world of commerce. Pierre Berton, though denounced, was also approved by the Christians he criticized. When, with more mildness, he wrote about sex in a secular journal, he was immediately dismissed. When *This Hour Has Seven Days*, a popular television program, dug into areas too controversial for the timid management of the Canadian Broadcasting Corporation, the inspirers of the program were fired. In the last case, the public's anger was aroused. There was a demand that some freedom be allowed somewhere in our society, and where better than to those who broadcast on public affairs? But the pressure of the unimaginative and uncontroversial is overwhelming and will probably prevail. You can't beat City Hall.

Except, perhaps, in a Church whose Mother is dead. I am not claiming that all is well, and I am aware – as so much of my mail points out – that original thought is rejected while the ideas of the fat cats are approved. At the same time, there is practical support for freedom of speech. John Robinson, who wrote the controversial *Honest to God*, is still a bishop. Thomas Altizer and William Hamilton still teach divinity. The Moderator of the United Church of Canada, Ernest Howse, survives the attacks of petty divinity students. When my own views were publicly (and legitimately) challenged by certain theological professors from Wycliffe and Trinity Colleges – and there followed some pitiful witch-hunts in the diocese of Toronto – there was immediate support for my right to state where I thought the problems of modern Christianity lay from the Primate, from the principal of a leading theological seminary, from the Executive of the General Board of Religious Education, and from many individual Christians. All this was very significant because very few of those who supported me at that time agreed with the views I was then expressing. Certainly, some of our Executive disagreed strongly with them; yet they publicly declared the need to allow freedom of expression. Their statement is worth reprinting and, I would suggest, worth imitating by the worlds of business, commerce, and education.

With regard to the controversy over statements made by the Reverend Ernest Harrison in the daily press, the Executive Committee of the General Board of Religious Education wishes to make certain points clear:

1. In the present state of theological ferment, as indeed at all times, it is one of the functions of an educator to challenge accepted opinions and formulations and to focus the problems of his day as sharply as he can.

2. While Mr. Harrison, like any other staff member, does not as an individual speak officially on behalf of the Department or the Church, at the same time he has the right and the responsibility as a member of the Department and the Church to speak his mind.

3. Mr. Harrison reflects the particular doubt and ferment and questioning that are widespread today in all the churches, together with a deep desire for a restatement of traditional teaching which will speak to the mind and heart of our age.

4. We do not believe that anyone is in a position to judge, on the basis of Mr. Harrison's statements in *The Globe and Mail* of January 15, 1966, whether Mr. Harrison is or is not beyond the general framework of the faith, life, and worship of the Anglican Church; and we do have confidence that he would feel obligated to resign from his office in the Church if he thought that he had moved beyond that framework.

This statement seemed to attract widespread support, though there was also much opposition. The opposition took various forms. The Reverend John McCausland of the Cowley Fathers expressed the dangers of being a public official and trying to speak personally at the same time. "Mr. Harrison holds an official position in the Church, and whether he likes it or not, he can't say anything about religious education or belief without binding the Church. In a manner of speaking, the officers at Church House are less able to act privately than a controversial bishop." And then there were those who advised firing. One whose letter was published in *The Canadian Churchman* (May 1966) was Randall E. Ivany of Red Deer, Alberta: "In a letter to the Bishop of Newfoundland, Dr. Seaborn, I asked him as Chairman of the

Board of the General Board of Religious Education why Harrison should not resign. The Bishop sent me a copy of the Statement of the Executive of the General Board of Religious Education and told me I should be satisfied. Well, I'm not satisfied. Moreover, if I'm going to stay in the Church and preach the Gospel of Christ, I'm going to be against Mr. Harrison's heresy." The least helpful comment came from J. Jocz, Professor of Theology at Wycliffe College, who wrote: "Should Mr. Harrison ever decide to leave Church House and the Department of Religious Education, may I suggest that a theological college would be an equally strategic position to pervert the Church." It was, interestingly, the only letter out of hundreds which thought of the matter in terms of perversion.

One of the most fascinating sidelights in the debate was the statement, frequently made, that somehow my views, expressed in a few short statements and a brief book,* could do great harm. Thus Randall Ivany: "I wonder if they realize how many are being driven outside the Church by the doubts spouted by Harrison and men like him."

I am, of course, not denying that people are leaving the Church, because this is a plain fact in all countries, whether they have Harrisons or not. Within the next decade, American and Canadian congregations will follow those in England, and it will be fortunate if they represent a third of their present level. But the reason? Here you have Mr. Ivany and clergy like himself devoting their lives to the people in their parishes, teaching them the Gospel, loving them, helping them to become themselves, to live the lives God would have them live. They know their people, they are in constant touch with them, they are on the spot. Into this powerful situation come a few thousand words "spouted" by a middle-aged priest in Toronto. Can a few words from a man they have probably never met, and whose portrait is not always presented as likeable, possibly undermine the deep-rooted faith of the churchgoer and make him turn his back on the lifetime of love and truth he has received in his parish? Can a few words of mine, acknowledged by these people to be self-evident heresy,

*Let God Go Free (Toronto: General Publishing Company; New York: Seabury Press, 1965).

11

disrupt the life-patterns of those who have only to turn to their rector for advice and guidance as to the real teaching of the Church? If indeed these men are right – that, in fact, some of their congregation actually weigh my words against the life-giving truth of the local Gospel and find the latter wanting – then I think there are other, more serious questions which Ivany might be asking.* Alongside these questions stand statements from the Executive, from local clergy and laymen (including the Calgary Diocese which Mr. Ivany represents), from the Primate and the Diocese of Edmonton, that freedom of expression must be allowed if the teaching of Christ means anything at all.

So here, in spite of exceptions, is one of the few segments in our society that permits great freedom. I need hardly say that it would not be permitted if Mother Church were still alive; and it is significant that those who yearn for the old days of the old doctrines are the ones who most loudly insist that views which are not to their liking should be suppressed and censored.

IV

It is, therefore, within a wide freedom that this book is being written. It has a practical purpose. In all the Churches of Europe and North America, large numbers of Christians part company, to a greater or lesser extent, with what has been called "the given" – that body of traditional ideas, beliefs, and practices inherited from the past.

Christians have parted company at many points. Some points – like the Virgin Birth or the succession of bishops – are trivial, leaving the main fabric intact and requiring merely small adjustments. Those who suffer from this mild attack of disenchantment include men who admit that they don't accept "all the clauses of the Creed" or concede, "I'm a bad Catholic on that, I guess." Other points, however, are more serious and occur at deeper levels. People who suffer from this major disenchantment, having

*Randall E. Ivany, a graduate engineer, *is* asking these questions and it is only fair to state here that he is well aware of the great problems of the contemporary Church. I think, however, that he misinterprets their cause.

parted company with the more serious doctrines and practices, have come to take an interest in what has been called the "New Theology." A wide variety of viewpoints is represented by this phrase, and it is no surprise to find that our new theologians are as dissimilar as the old, both in their cast of mind and their specific conclusions. Yet they share one common attitude: they believe very little, if any, of the "given," and they accept nothing merely on the say-so of former Christians.

The new theologians are accompanied by rapidly increasing numbers of laymen and clergy. How far down the road of rebellion against the "given" they move is a matter of personal conviction and pressure; but the direction is clear. No longer do they take fright when they find their doubts running deep. All major Christian denominations now include loyal members who do not believe in God, the Apostles' Creed, the doctrine of the Trinity, the divinity of Christ, the physical resurrection of Jesus, or in an after-life for themselves. They do not consider the Bible to be basically different in kind from other books, and they do not pray.

To other members of their denominations, to most clergy, and to nearly all bishops, such apparent negations put a Christian outside the fold. It is impossible, they insist, to be a Christian without accepting in some measure certain basic doctrines. When faced with those who do not agree with them, they sometimes reach down into the grab-bag of history and haul out the words "apostasy" and "heresy." Freedom of speech and belief is acknowledged, but this, they say, is going too far.

One of their chief complaints about the "New Theology" is that it is too negative. The retort to this is obvious: all theology is both positive and negative. The Old Theology, though it proclaimed many positive dicta concerning God, was highly negative concerning Man. An evangelist, commenting recently upon the "Death of God" theology, declared "God's not dead; we are." In doing so, he took a similar attitude to that of the Anglican Prayer Book, which leaves man little dignity and no virtue except that which is conceded to him in response to his loyal attention to certain obligations. Conversely, a New Theologian, like John Robinson, while he appears to be negative in that he attacks the normal practices of Christian worship, is in reality affirming a wider description of prayer, which ensures its application to all men and implies a practice more real. He who saves his life shall lose it; and we shall never understand prayer until we get rid of it.

Yet the accusation that the New Theology is negative must be taken seriously. In writing the following book, I have tried to avoid negation whenever possible, but much remains. I am deeply convinced that Mother Church led us far away from Christ; and I am glad that we are free of her. I cannot write of the new freedoms within Christianity, of the positive goals now made possible, of the chance we at last have of coming close to Jesus Christ, without noting what I believe to be the negative attitude of the Church in the past and the restrictive nature of her methods and doctrines. Yet I have tried to keep these notes to a minimum.

In order to do so I have made certain assumptions. I assume that traditional dogmatic theology is no longer relevant to the lives of many thousands of Christians, for whom there is no chance of returning to the old Creeds, no matter how well argued. No implications are made beyond this. I assume that traditional theology was devised and refined by wise, clever, and sincere men. They made their teaching relevant to the people of their day and, if it is not relevant to us, then that reflects in no way upon their work. Nor does it reflect badly on those who today hold those traditional notions to be true. Professor E. L. Mascall, to name one, is a highly intelligent writer and thinker who sees the old ideas as relevant to his own life and who is read warmly by those who agree with him. If they truly believe him, they are wise in their choice. There are many mansions available, and there is no need for the occupants of any one of them to deny the existence or the integrity of others. In other words, this book is intended in no way to undermine the faith of anyone.

Nor is it an attempt to help renew or revitalize the Church as an institution in our society. I do not care whether the Church, in its present state, survives or disappears. I do care whether or not there are congregations of Christians whose life pulses because they meet together. Like Harvey Cox, I feel that what is required is a renewal of the world and that the Church may, or may not, prove to be important in such a renewal. If it plays a part, then it is justified. If it does not, then it may as well join the temples of Adonis as a scholar's memory and a tourist's holiday.

Mother Church is dead; but her children remain. To those who wish to bring Mother back to life, those who are unable or unwilling to accept the freedom and responsibility which have come to them upon her death, this book is useless. It has nothing to say, one way or the other, to the person who feels that, in order to be a Christian, he must accept certain tenets as matters of Faith. It is written, rather, to give assurance, from within the community of Christians, to those who – members of a denomination or not – feel no such need and are encountering problems because they do not. They accept the trend of the New Theology, they admire such men as Bishop Robinson, and they think that he speaks for them. They feel that they are coming to understand who Jesus was and what he represented; to understand what men are and how they may become one race; to understand the Gospel in completely new ways which really make it sound like Good News. Yet they are accused by fellow churchmen, especially clergy, of being disloyal; they are told that they ought to get out of the Church; that they are no longer entitled to call themselves Christian.

They are trapped. For, in spite of the loud cries of heresy, they do not feel like heretics. They feel like Christians. They feel that they are as much entitled to membership in their Church as those who condemn them. This book tries to establish that they have every right to call themselves Christian and to remain members of their denomination. In simple terms, this book says: You will be attacked, but stay as long as you wish to stay. You may feel lonely, but there is much support all over the Church for you. If you wish to go, go. God (in whatever terms) is everywhere. But do not be driven out. Mother Church is dead, and any threats that are sounded in her name are idle ones.

CHAPTER II

꿜

A Many-Splendoured Society

꿜

I

Liverpool 1932. Alex Woods sat listening patiently to his grand-mother, his mind tightly screened, his ears tuned for the words which would signify that she would soon stop. His reply had been ready before she began.

The old lady spat on the flat-iron which had made no mark on the white shirt she was pressing. She ran it across her flat bosom. "The bloody thing's gone cold," she muttered, walking over to the gas stove to heat it up. "I've told your dear, sweet mother once, and I've told her ten hundred times, it's all this schooling that's the trouble. Overwork your brain and it'll rot like any other part of you. It's the doctor you should be seeing as well as the good Father. A grandson of mine saying that a Protestant might be right! May the Good Lord and his holy saints have pity on you."

He pinched his thick, prickly trousers between his fingers. "Montague Burton, the Tailor of Taste. 37/6d." Generations of Irish-family discipline kept him glued to his seat, his voice held at a respectful volume. "I only said I wanted to marry Phyllis. When you told me she'd have to change her religion, I simply said she'd make her own mind up, and that was my opinion, too."

"There's no call to shiver," replied the old lady. "You always were a bit on the nesh side. You'd best take off that thin under-wear you've got on, and I'll give you a pair of your grandad's wool. She's a beautiful girl, mind. Not one of your common things, their lipstick and all." She stopped abruptly. She liked the speech which had flashed through her mind, but she felt compassion for the young man in front of her and resisted the luxury of delivering it. She sat down beside him and lowered her voice, laying her hand on his knee. "Look you here, Alex boy, I don't say the Good Lord doesn't care for them Protestant heretics. Father Dominic said it at Mass last Sunday, and quite right he was to tell those young whipper-snappers off for making all that din. God's love is infinite, he said, and even Protestants may be saved. But you've got to live with her, all day and all night. When that bedroom door shuts, it shuts the world out and you two alone together, until the Good Lord gives you the family. She's a Protestant, remember that, boy, a Protestant – not just for the wedding, but minute after minute until you die."

Alex sat in silence. She had not chosen her words idly. He looked back along the years that had made the word Protestant so terrifying. Protestants were error against truth, cruelty against kindness, hatred against love. They were obstinate, they denied the Holy Ghost, knowing the truth – for who could fail to see such objective reality? – yet rejecting it. Faced with the inescapable logic of a Jesuit father, only a deep-rooted desire to reject the living God could make a man refuse to believe the clearly proved facts. In large numbers, before your very eyes, they did reject. His mind tore down the long fires at the corners of the street, the loud shouts as King Billy went up in flames at one end, the Pope at the other. Especially the Pope. That was what hurt. Everyone knew that King Billy was a scoundrel and a tyrant, a man who ought to be burned in effigy, like Guy Fawkes every fifth of November. A penny for the guy and, if it was King Billy, what the heck? Teachers said Guy Fawkes was really a Catholic fighting for the true faith; but you could be broadminded and burn them both if you wanted. Weren't they both men? But the Pope was different. He wasn't just a mortal; he was the vicar of Christ, a man from God. Burn the Pope, as the Protestants did, and you burned God.

His thoughts began to tumble over each other as the limitless incidents, the scraps of teaching, and the emotional hurts brought blood hatred to the word Protestant. And yet, biting into the

17

flood of events, were those queer little incidents, only seconds in length, which had thrown doubt on the whole. The snowballs. Three or four times a winter, the Liverpool streets would be covered with a few inches of perilous snow, soft and ready for fight. Only the scared were late for school on such days, when Saint Augustine's went to war with Litherstone Road Elementary. The results were always the same. The proddy-dogs, faced with defeat, put stones inside their snowballs. Later, during the morning, bloody Catholic foreheads would be paraded and inspected; and the wickedness of those who would not play fair would be proclaimed. God was praised for – in spite of Protestant cheating – Catholic right had triumphed and Saint Augustine's had won the fight. Again. Every time.

It was years later, now an adolescent, that Alex entered his deep and hurtful friendship with John Heller. At one o'clock after midnight, and two bottles of wine, they tugged out their hatred and hostility.

"What I can't understand," mumbled John, "and I'm not whining, mind you, but it's just this, wack: why did youse Catholics put stones in your snowballs? It didn't seem right, like. I know we always beat you; but you might have taken it more sporting."

And so the incidents had flowed, trivial yet always building up to a realization that, in order to identify with a Protestant, all you had to do was to think like a Catholic. When you actually got to know them, they were just the same as you were. They had the same emotions, the same deep faiths and doubts, the same loves and hates, the same pleasure at laying a girl and the same guilt afterwards. The same everything. They just played in a different part of the yard. It wasn't a question of truth, or love, or anything absolute at all. He remembered looking across at John Heller. You bastard, he thought, and God help us! What our religion does, separating us and making us hate, and feel guilty when we love. All that matters is that we are both men. But he had said nothing.

His ear, picking up a signal, warned him that his grandmother was nearing the end of a speech. He dragged himself away from the past and John Heller. "It may be right," she was saying. "A Protestant may be a Christian. I'm not going to say one thing and

I'm not going to say the other. But, Alex, where's it all going to end? If Protestants are right, what about these atheists and agnostics and all the heathen on the other side of the world? You start saying your Phyllis may be right, next thing you'll be saying that terrible Bernard Shaw is right, and soon it'll be the devil's a fine gentleman like Bishop Downey, and a darling man he is, too."

II

Where will it all end? Thirty-five years later, as we move to the end of the sixties, we are beginning to see where it all ends. I have told of three characters in a certain background because that is how the events took place and, though the names are changed, the details are not. The facts of human life being what they are, you may interchange the labels any way you will. As Alex discovered, all you had to do to identify with a man of a different faith was to be yourself and simply move into a different part of the schoolyard. Whatever clear-sightedness was to be found in Roman Catholics was to be found in Anglicans, Methodists, and every brand of Protestantism, in agnostics, atheists, scoffers, and unbelievers without exception. Similarly, whatever parts of our minds were closed were closed whoever we were. As we look back, we can see that the Wells's and the Huxley's were every bit as creative and destructive, open and dogmatic, sighted and blind, wise and foolish, forward- and backward-looking as the Belloc's and Chesterton's, the Lewis's and the Sayers's.

Nor was this spectrum limited to the cold, dirty iron and gloomy colourations of a depressed England. The man who lost his larynx when Dixie Dean scored a last-minute goal for Everton against Liverpool was the same man who lost it when Dizzie Dean struck out the last man up for the Dodgers. The man who lectured on theology at Downside in England was the same man who lectured at an Episcopal Seminary in the United States and a United Church College in Canada.

Faith and unfaith, knowledge and ignorance, science and superstition, were, in the thirties, showing themselves as characteristics of all religions and non-religions, all walks of life, all types of person, all countries and all cities within them, all human beings and the Jekyll and Hyde Unlimited which made them up.

Today in Canada, the United States, and England, this pluralism – implicit, as Alex's grandmother detected, in the discovery that a person of an opposite religion could also be right – is now an accepted fact of our national lives. It is very good, this many-splendoured society in which we find ourselves. No longer do we feel the need for a single focus to our lives, a single God, a single true religion, a single philosophy, or a single truth. In spite of the fears of those who dreaded the arrival of pluralism, the result has not been chaos. The greatest artists, writers, scientists, and philosophers of our generation have been drawn from all types of men, from those who believe in a single God and a single absolute Truth, to those who do not accept absolutes at all, who do not believe in God. And the latter are not chaotic in their creativity.

On the level of the average man, it is equally obvious that pluralism produces the same wide range of activity and philosophy as any other -ism, including the Christian. There is no way of perceiving, from the outward signs of discipline and chaos, whether a man believes in God or not, accepts absolutes or not, follows a relativist morality or not. Experience shows that Christianity is one way, but only one way, to live the good life. In sermons, articles, and speeches at Synods, many a religious leader has deplored the changes in our way of thinking about God and the Church and, in doing so, predicted that immorality and promiscuity will result. Yet our lives, as they pass, show such fears to be groundless, though they may be legitimate for the proclaimer in his own private life. A simple test may be used to demonstrate this. If I tell you that John Smith has stolen from a supermarket, been discovered in bed with another man's wife, has libelled a fellow-citizen unjustly, or has murdered a man, can you, from these events, deduce what his religion is, or if he has any?

The claim is constantly made that religion is the bedrock of morals and the good life. This has some merit, but the claim is inadequate. We may nowadays say that *any* philosophy of life, no matter how well or badly articulated, no matter how logical or illogical, emotional or unemotional, objective or subjective, so long as it is sincerely based, may be a bedrock of morals and the good life.

III

For the religious person, especially a member of a church congregation, the realization that he does not have to believe in only one faith comes as a great relief. For generations, the plea for a single focus to our religious life has run as a constant thread through our scriptures, prayerbooks, catechisms, sermons, and hymns. One God. One Lord, One Faith, One Baptism. One God and Father of all. The Church's One Foundation. It is *the* Faith which is referred to, *the* Faith in *the* Truth and *the* God. Absolute Love, Absolute Goodness, Absolute Truth, Absolute Purity. One. If only we could identify ourselves with this one, true, good, beautiful, and pure God, then we would indeed be knit together into one race, one church, one fold, one flock, with one shepherd.

Hearing this message every Sunday, most churchgoers spent the rest of their lives denying or ignoring it among people whose practices denied or ignored it. Our cities, suburbs, villages, and hamlets were dotted with churches whose varied architecture, ways of worship, and ecclesiastical government paid tribute to a diverse interpretation of this one God, one Truth, one Goodness, and one Beauty. We were more surprised than joyful to discover a neighbour who went to our church or even held remotely the same philosophy of life. Unless we took to a ghetto in the fashion of Jehovah's Witnesses, or little groups within our major denominations, and met only with those of like mind to ourselves, we learned to work and live with our neighbours whatever their point of view. We learned to respect the convictions of others, and felt less and less need to convert the agnostic to Christianity or the Christian to agnosticism. We learned, through experience, that conversion and communication cannot live happily together. Where conversion begins, communication ceases.

And so there developed what is in danger of becoming a new

orthodoxy: the philosophy of live and let live. You go your way, says the New Citizen, and I'll go mine. Everyone is entitled to his own opinion, and mine are no better than anyone else's. At a deeper level, this pluralism takes upon itself a more subtle interplay of different ways of learning, changing, discovering, and behaving. It is not merely that Smith is willing to let Jones follow his way, while Smith follows his. The two have now learned to live and work together on the same human or community projects without their differing views leading to a division between them. Though highly relevant to his conduct and attitudes, a man's religion need not intrude upon his relationships with others and, when it does, animosity, separation, and segregation are seen as the denial of what it stands for. So it is that the Christian sees his Christianity denied rather than affirmed, when he tries to convert his neighbour, because such conversion normally works to the detriment of their relationship; he sees that relationship fulfilled when he says little of his own creed, and that little for the purpose of sharing with the other and helping him identify himself. The result is that religion is no longer excluded from discussion in polite society. On the contrary, it is now welcomed more warmly than for many a generation because its base has been broadened. No longer can anyone successfully adopt the role of knowing best or having a better road to the truth than his neighbour.

It is this popular pluralism, practised by nearly every citizen, which embarrasses the churchgoer. From Monday to Saturday he has no problem, whether he adopts the live-and-let-live, the let-us-dialogue-with-those-who-are-different, or the so-long-as-we-love-what-the-heck approach. But, on Sunday, if he is a member of a Church, he takes part in a ritual which denies the basis upon which he has built his normal life. His prayer book, if he is an Anglican, sets up only one group of people as truly faithful and, even when it is compassionately disposed to outsiders, urges not only that they be changed, but that it is the Christian duty of the insider to change them. Unless he contrives to detach himself from the words which are said (and many churchgoers possess this happy knack), problems are created.

A good example is the Church's attitude towards the Jews.

During his everyday life, the Christian is learning at last to work alongside Jews. It is a slow process even now, because anti-Semitism is wide-spread in our society among all types of people, whether religious or not. But the direction of change is clear. Many, perhaps most, churchgoers are learning that the Jew is a human being – no more and no less. That he has his virtues and faults like anyone else. That he is just as honest and dishonest as the Gentile, just as clever and stupid, and so on.

As a result, his life away from the Church is one of growing co-operation. He works alongside Jews on community projects. He attends educational seminars at a Synagogue. He learns to respect dietary laws and is fascinated to find that some Jews do not observe them. As he does so, he discovers that the Jew is no longer looking at him with suspicion, that the ancient fears, though still alive, are allayed.

Then he goes to Church on Good Friday, one of the most sacred days in the Christan year. Until recently, he prayed to God: "Have mercy upon all Jews, Turks, infidels, and heretics, and take from them all ignorance, hardness of heart, and contempt of thy Word." In 1959, the Canadian Church made an attempt to correct this piece of horrifying arrogance, but the timidity of the correction is possibly as hurtful. In the seventeenth century, society at large shared with the Catholic Church its assumption that the Church alone possessed the truth about God, and that Jews were obviously beyond the pale, the rightful recipients of the wrath of God by virtue of their killing of Him on Good Friday. Today, society at large knows better, that the Jews were far from denying God. Yet we still pray: "Have mercy upon the Jews, thine ancient people, and upon all who reject and deny thy Son; take from them all ignorance, hardness of heart, and contempt of thy word; and so fetch them home, blessed Lord. . . ." A friend, a rabbi, said to me, when I told him of the change we had made, "Big deal." He was to use the same phrase when faced with the Second Vatican Council which, realizing the irresponsibility of the former Christian attitude towards the Jews, could still not bring itself to pronounce the Church's sinfulness in the matter in clear and unmistakeable terms. Grudgingly, as it appears to so many Jews, the Council acknowledged merely that the modern Jew is not a god-killer. The battle for Christian charity towards the Jews continues, but what a chance was missed by Rome to chop short the struggle by years!

This contrast, between the everyday life of the worshipper and that implied in his Church Services, is not restricted to the treatment of the Jews. Every aspect of the Christian's relationship with his fellow men is affected. His daily experiences inform him that his neighbour is as good a man as he is, and that their highest aim is to love and understand each other. He fails, but he recognizes both the aim and the failure. On Sundays, however, his neighbour becomes fodder for the Church; to be changed, converted, made over into a pattern which may be offensive to him but which is presumed to be for his good.

The assumption of the prayer book is clear: there are two communities, those who are saved and those who are not. It is the duty of the first to convert the second, and God's help is necessary to do this. The definition of the two communities is, to some extent, in terms of the good life; but it is mostly in terms of concepts – what one believes about God, Christ, the Trinity, and the Sacraments. A man is not to be judged by his fruits so much as the basic tenets of his belief. The Christian may live a harmful life, and must seek forgiveness, but he is still a Christian. The atheist may show all the fruits of a deep Christian belief, but he remain an atheist. It is still the duty of the first to convert the second.

If the churchgoer really believed this, nothing would stop him from trying at every turn to win his non-agreeing neighbours to the Truth, no matter what the cost. In the past, this was the agreed position. The Crusaders destroyed the Infidel; Mary Tudor burned Latimer and Ridley; Elizabeth I beheaded Mary Stuart; a wing of the Anglican Low Church imprisoned a nineteenth-century High Churchman for putting candles on an altar; the governors of a Roman Catholic institution of learning dismissed non-conforming staff . . . and so on, examples without end.

The same phenomenon shows itself today. If a churchgoer – whether Roman Catholic, Anglican, United at one end; or Pentecostal, Seventh Day Adventist or Jehovah's Witness at the other – feels that he possesses the truth about the one God, then he has no option but to change and to insist on changing, by whatever means are practicable, the lives of those around him who do not share his convictions. In practice, he protects this position by creating a ghetto in which he can preserve his agreed-upon beliefs to his own satisfaction. The outsider looks on, pays tribute to the great faith of the zealous believer, and takes care to steer clear of his narrow-mindedness.

IV

Sympathetic with the outsider is the average churchgoer. He does not believe that Christ alone can lead mankind to maturity. He does not believe that the agnostic or atheist is any worse than he is; he does not see them as heathens, and he makes no effort to convert them. Apart, therefore, from the odd invitation to attend such safe occasions as a tea or a dance, a Christmas or Easter Service, he leaves his neighbour to his own philosophy, shares his ideas with him from time to time, and relegates churchgoing to where he feels it belongs – to Sunday, and to those others who desire, for whatever motive, to attend.

This is a positive and creative attitude, and those churchgoers who acquire it are growing daily. But it is not free from an uneasy conscience. A preacher, anxious to intensify the guilty feelings of his congregation, need only draw attention to the undeniable gap between the claims made in church and the practice of the congregation during the week. A popular preacher, now a bishop, used this device successfully on many occasions. He talked about his great experiences as an evangelist in London, building up vivid pictures of the great crowds that gathered to scoff, observe, listen, and sometimes believe. Having painted the hot gatherings, the heady atmosphere, the stink and the grime, he then mentioned the challenges that used to pour out of the crowd. It was necessary, he said, for the evangelist to answer these questions, or the Christian cause would be lost. He then paused and illustrated the need by quoting a typical question, usually drawn from one of the more abstruse passages of the Old Testament, a question like, "How many children did Seth have?" It was a safe assumption that none of the congregation would be able to answer. The preacher then quickly moved into his real task, to stir up their feelings of guilt so that he could sell his own particular message. As the congregation indicated, by an uneasy silence that they could not answer his question, he quickly established his conclusion. If you cannot answer every question put to you about the Bible, he demanded, what use are you for responding to the unbeliever?

Indeed – and what use is the Bible at all if it is used at so idiotic and trivial a level? But the guilt of the churchgoer was by now so raw that he had moved beyond consulting his common-sense. The preacher had him at his mercy. There was a plain inconsistency between the Sunday philosophy and that of his daily life: surely he must have failed in his faith.

But there was another possible reaction: that the weekday method was closer to modern religious life, more vital, and (whatever the word may mean) nearer to God than the Sunday method. This decision has been made by at least a third of the populations of Canada and the United States, and about four-fifths of England's. Knowing that his weekday life has a reasonable and potentially valuable basis, knowing that the ways of his agnostic neighbours are as good or bad as his own, the Christian – challenged on Sunday to make a choice between the two lives – has already made it. He does not go to Church except on state occasions.

But this is no solution for large numbers of churchgoers. Agreeing that there is a difference between the two patterns of life set out, and feeling strongly that the worldly one is potentially the right one for him, he still wishes to attend Church for many reasons, some of which I will discuss in Chapter VIII. He may, however, take confidence in the fact that more and more church-goers, though still a minority, and not represented at all in the centres of ecclesiastical power and finance, have already rejected the portrait of life offered in our present prayer books, church services, and sermons. They live in hope that these will change, especially the sermons. For a while, they are willing to close their ears and gather strength from their growing conviction that they do not, as Christians, have to believe that there is a single faith, a single core to their being, a single authority in any sphere, or a single foundation to their lives.

It is, of course, constantly suggested that pluralism, with its denial of such a unity, will inevitably lead to chaos, and that relativism, with its denial of universal truths, will inevitably lead to insecurity. Take away the rock on which my life is built and there will be nothing left to hold me from sinking in the quicksands around me. Rock the boat and we shall all be in danger of drowning. Destroy one corner of my faith and who knows whether any of it will survive? Take away my belief in God and his Church, and I shall have no basis for living the good life or seeking the truth. Kill my Mother and I too will die.

We now have enough evidence to show that these fears are unjustified. Perhaps the most significant is the scientific, largely because it is so much an admired, almost idolized, part of modern man's existence. In the nineteenth century, science was as dogmatic as any religion. It knew best. It could analyze accurately and predict the natural outcome of events. Like Mother Church, it believed in law. The twentieth century has shot the law to pieces. Science no longer knows best, and the dogmatism is at an end. One of the most familiar examples of this change can be found in the definitions that scientists offer of Light. Charles H. Townes, in an essay entitled "The Convergence of Science and Religion," in *Think* magazine (March-April 1966) which deals with this change, writes:

> Many of the philosophical and conceptional bases of science have in fact been disturbed and revolutionized. The poignancy of these changes can be grasped only through sampling them. For example, the question of whether light consists of small particles shot out by light sources or wave disturbances originated by them had been debated for some time by the great figures of science. The question was finally settled in the early nineteenth century by brilliant experimentation which could be thoroughly interpreted by theory. The experiments told scientists of the time that light was unequivocally a wave and not particles. But about 1900, other experiments turned up which showed just as unequivocally that light is a stream of particles rather than waves. Thus physicists were presented with a deeply disturbing paradox. Its solution took several decades, and was only accomplished

in the mid-1920's by the development of a new set of ideas known as quantum mechanics. . . . In retrospect, it is not at all surprising that the study of matter on the atomic scale has taught us new things, and that some are inconsistent with ideas which previously had seemed so clear. Physicists today believe that light is neither precisely a wave nor a particle, but both, and we were mistaken in even asking the question, "Is light a particle or is it a wave?" It can display both properties. So can all matter.

In other words, the two explanations offered (there will be more in the future) may be mutually exclusive, but may both be true.

The same approach can be made to religious questions. For certain purposes, God may be described in ways offered by St. Thomas and the modern orthodox theologians; for other purposes, he may be described in ways offered by Paul Tillich and John Robinson; for still others, he may be described in ways suggested by Thomas Altizer and William Hamilton. They cannot all be joined together in one system. There is no obvious way, to say the least, of conjoining St. Thomas' expert analysis of the attributes of God, Tillich's demonstration of God as ultimate concern, and Hamilton's proclamation that the God who was once alive is now dead. The present suggestion – leaving aside whether such a conjunction may one day be made – is that there is no need to make it. Different ways, different analyses, different conclusions. That each individually may be challenged is obvious. If I find St. Thomas of little value, I must say so. If I find Altizer offensive, I must say so. And we can challenge and argue. Behind these arguments there may legitimately lie an assumption which church people are now encouraged to make: whatever the specific complaints and difficulties, there is every reason to suppose that all three schools are right.

Or, to take a briefer illustration: Just as scientists discovered that they had hindered themselves when they asked a question in the form: "Is light a particle or is it a wave?" so theologians may hinder themselves when they ask a question in the form: "Was Jesus born of a Virgin or of two parents?"

All this adds a new dimension to such activities as listening to sermons, taking part in liturgies, singing hymns, saying creeds, and attending synods. The sermon, which means so much to the preacher, may mean nothing to me, a little to my wife, and everything to the young man in front. I need not suppose that only one of these views is right, or even more right than another. They may all be correct. The young theological student believes that Jesus was born of a Virgin, my son thinks it may be historically correct but can take it or leave it, my daughter thinks the whole idea is nonsense. I need not suppose that any of these views is correct or even attempt to synthesize them.

V

So far, I have been talking about pluralism as it appears in our society: a phenomenon accepted daily by most citizens. Those who change hats and attend church on Sunday find themselves embarrassed. A minority of those who attend accept pluralism as the more creative doctrine. It is a minority that gathers strength daily and which will, within a few years, be heard in the ruling councils of the Church.

We can, however, take a further step – into ourselves as individuals. That we are not single entities has been known since the dawn of mankind and is dramatized in folk tales which – like the werewolf or the vampire – entertain generation after generation because they touch those deep-rooted convictions that alone can scratch our nerves. We know that we cannot be simply explained, and we know that a good man hides an evil one as surely as an evil man hides a good one.

Yet the simple dualism of good and evil which lies in all of us is not enough. Anyone who has passed through a psycho-drama group or an exercise in group therapy no matter how simple will have discovered that he is a strange, vibrating creation which has no simple or single explanation. Dr. Johann B. Metz calls this fact of our complicated and inconsistent being "that remarkable pluralism of consciousness which all of these produce for the individual person: the fact that man must live more and more out of the most varied tendencies and impulses, such that he can no longer bring them into a spiritually controllable unity which he can see altogether."

This is well said, and it sums up the instinctive feeling of so many modern men. Even when they have made no excursions into the territory of psychological analysis or therapy, they understand that there is no single explanation to human conduct; that motives are never simple or single-minded; that actions are impossible to explain in such categories as good or bad, right or wrong, except on the most superficial lines; that I can never know you, and you can never know me, and neither of us can know ourselves fully. However far we travel, there is more ahead. A modern man can accept, without fear of collapsing into chaotic misery, that he is a living mass of many philosophies, many religions, and many atheisms, and that many of these are inconsistent with each other. I am a believer one moment, a disbeliever the next; a lover one second, a hater the next; emotional one moment, rational the next – and not just one moment after another, but all of these at the same time. At the very moment I love, at that moment I also hate; at the very moment I believe in God, at that moment I hate him and love him and disbelieve in him. I wish he were there and am convinced that he is and that he is not. This is how I live. It does not sound very sensible set out in words; it certainly does not lend itself to a series of logical syllogisms. But it is life, nonetheless, and we know it. What modern discoveries have done is to give us confidence as we live with ourselves as we really are. Discovering that we are all an amalgam of contradictory and bewildering characteristics, we do not seek to escape, but to live.

Far from becoming a deviant, the individual pluralist often lives a disciplined life, more disciplined in many respects than that of his One-God neighbour. Thus, it is now well-proven by many researchers – not to mention the letters-to-the-editor columns in the daily newspapers – that religious people who believe in One God are *more* apt to support capital punishment, the imprisonment of those who have done wrong, and the punishment of crime than irreligious people. This is not unexpected. The belief that we must have a single foundation to our lives means that a bad action is a bad action. To such a believer, the notion that criminals are sick men sounds vague and woolly. The believer has divided humanity into the godly and the ungodly, the Church, on the one hand, the world, the flesh, and the devil, on the other. To him the idea that we may never make a judgment about someone else's sins seems offensive. To the man of single mind, the homosexual is an aberrant who should be dealt with severely by social ostracism, punishment, or deprivation of liberty. When the man of single mind finds himself a member of a group which is willing to pursue the members' real natures as persons, he often becomes angry and goes home. The discovery that he is no better than the men whose sinful ways of life he has decried is too horrible for him to face. It is one thing to say glibly that all men have sinned; it is another to see that the difference between himself and the homosexual, the drug pusher, or the prostitute is too slight for comment.

A recognition of this pluralism of consciousness is a step in maturity. It denies nothing of the love that is poured out in the name of those who believe in the One True God. It simply extends it to all and so becomes Catholic. It takes away nothing from the narrow way to salvation, but extends it to Jews, Buddhists, Hindus, and Moslems who have suddenly become our next-door neighbours. Modern man finds that he can only be truly himself when he recognizes all his neighbours to be as fully human as he is. The whole world has now entered his life, and no group of people can any more be excluded, denigrated, or converted.

VI

It is now, after he has survived the attacks of those motivated by creeds, and has found his ideas well established among church-goers, that the pluralist Christian needs to be careful. An acutely dangerous moment occurs when he suddenly feels that the tide is running his way. This is a fact in which he may well rejoice; but, unless he is wary, he may overlook the equally certain fact that this direction will itself one day change, that his present convictions will become the target for attacks, and that those attacks will be justified. If he is careless, he will come to believe that pluralism is the end of the trail, the solution of his problems and those of his neighbour.

If pluralism becomes a New Orthodoxy, it will work against the maturity it now represents. One of Jesus' most penetrating observations was that the Strengthener would lead men into all truth. The Faith, the Bible, the Torah, Christ himself are steps on the way, not the goal or end. There is no final revelation, a discovery that we most dislike making. We can see the delusions of other people; it is more difficult to see our own. Bertrand Russell perceives with crystal clarity the absurdities of Christian dogmatism; he ignores his own. The determinist exempts himself from his theories. The relativist sits lightly by the fact that his own ideas are relative. The agnostic feels that he knows at least one truth. The atheist does not demand the rigorous proof of God's non-being that he demands of his being. And the pluralist might think that he has at last reached full maturity. He would be wrong; there is more maturing and changing ahead, and we must be ready for it.

It is, in other words, naïve to suppose that somehow pluralism will work a magic which traditional Christianity has failed to work. There is no magic in any religion, philosophy, or science. They all carry with them the same ingredients, the minds and imaginations of men. Men mature and change, but they do so slowly, and there are no short cuts. At the moment, the pluralist may, if he wishes, live in a dream world. He is like the European about to emigrate to the wealth and security of the New World. All seems good and challenging. When he arrives at his new home, however, he will soon discover that he has dragged himself along with his hopes. The problems which beset him in Europe will beset him in America and, though he matures and grows, there will be no alchemical transmutation. If he dreams that America will neutralize or remove the weaknesses and neuroses which lie within him, he will be disillusioned.*

At the moment, the pluralist can point to the defects of Christendom with great certainty, because his own philosophy has not yet had time to build up a backlog of error to compare with that built up by the Church. Harvey Cox lists six facts which the

---

*I am not implying that America is more mature than Europe. The illustration would do just as well the other way around, with an American about to leave for Europe.

Church cannot ignore in the twentieth century. The fourth of these is the "self-invalidation of the Christian claim to produce a basis for order and morality," and he uses as a classical example the concentration camps at Auschwitz. Here, as he says, we see the end result of the theology of Christendom which taught that Jews were god-killers, members of a group that opposed God against his champions, the servants of Mother Church. The philosophy outlined in *Mein Kampf*, though pressed into new and horrifying areas, was a religious statement in the same tradition as the attacks made by former Christians upon "Jews, Turks, Infidels, and Heretics." Furthermore, the tragedy of Hitler was enacted in a country which had long been one of the leading centres of Christian theology. It was here that some of the greatest thinkers within Christendom found their home. A Christian people, reared for centuries within the Christian ethic, found themselves led by a baptized Christian into one of the fiercest of all possible indictments of the human race. It was the final curtain for Christian polemic.

As yet, there has been no pluralist or secular Auschwitz. It is tempting to hope that there never will be, that the good-will built into the new ways of life will, in some magical way, wipe out the horrors of the past while preserving its charity. This is an absurd dream which will be shattered unless we see it as a dream. G. K. Chesterton, fighting a last-ditch stand for Mother Church, declared: "It is not that Christianity has been tried and found wanting; it has never been tried." Within his own terminology, he was right. But Christendom *had* been tried and *had* failed. The Good News remains to be tried, and Christian pluralism is, at the moment, the most fruitful way. It remains, however, the work of men, the same human race which produced Belsens at the heart of Christendom. No doubt, one day, some critic will declare: "It is not that pluralism has been tried and found wanting; it has never been tried." For in every religion or philosophy, there is an ideal that is never achieved. The supporter looks to the ideal and, when its chief exponents prove cruel, declares that these exponents are not really true followers. The opponent looks to the cruelty and feels that the aberrations destroy the ideal.

The facts, however, remain as they are. The Christian Gospel was, and is, a noble way of life which did not move beyond a hopeful theory. As practised in Christendom, it failed, and Mother Church, corrupt and decayed, is at last seen to be dead. Pluralism takes up some of the hope, though it no longer sees Christ as essential. It will, in time, face its own distortions and has no more guarantee of solving our problems than any previous way.

Moreover, we already have enough evidence to perceive what the future may hold. There is enough misuse by one human being of another, enough control of our lives by the military outlook (in all of us), enough promiscuity and wilful hurt, enough mugging, torturing, and cruel slaying, enough Viet-Nam's, to suggest that we would be living in a world of unreality if we thought that there would never be a Belsen or Auschwitz built in the context of a pluralist way of life. Hitler acted as he did, was followed, and was opposed within a Christian context; his followers acted because they were human, and were opposed by others who did so because of their humanity. It has been the tragedy of Christendom to offer so much and to give so little. There is no reason to suppose that any of our present or future alternatives will be free of the same danger.

These weaknesses in pluralism are familiar to the orthodox and are used constantly by such men as Michael Ramsay to imply that, in the face of such a danger, surely we should return to the securities of established Christendom. The quest for such securities is hopeless. When change comes, it is never a reversal to a previous position. Old religions have moments of great influence long after their deaths, but they never return to life. Traditional Christianity will fare no better than the Greek mythological religions. It will know moments of great influence far into the future; but, once decayed, it will never come back. New modes of life and maturity will shape themselves in patterns which, delighting neither the orthodox nor the radical, neither the monist nor the pluralist, will shock both. The arrival of pluralism as a popular way of life has already thrown together into unity various segments of the Christian Church which were formerly enemies; the successors of pluralism may well produce equally strange bedfellows.

But this is in the future. The present is clear enough. Pluralism is here and it is here strongly. It is the pattern for secular man, and it is good. Many men, knowing this, have moved out of the established Church; many more will do so. Those who remain find themselves in an apparent minority, loudly denounced from pulpit and church papers. Yet enough of them now perceive that they are in the pattern of the future and will remain in the Church to see that future take shape. It is part of the fear expressed in the latter section of this chapter that, when it does take shape, we may find the bishops of the day denouncing whatever it is that will be challenging the world to change once more. Even when we adjust to the fact that an old doctrine has collapsed, we still cling to the hope that our new one will surely remain for ever. In the realm of pluralism, the hope is as much a delusion as in any other.

CHAPTER III

So There Is No God

I

If Mother Church is dead, we cannot long delay asking the question: What about God? She offered herself as his one true agent; and we must ask if this God, in whose name she acted, has also died. The question is one that threatens Christians most deeply. There was, after all, much that was to be admired in the conviction that God was alive and spoke through his appointed mouthpiece. We cannot help but feel a fierce nostalgia. If only this God were, indeed, with us, to give security and safety; if only we still knew this strong rock upon which we could stand without fear unto all eternity. If only . . . but it is impossible. Once man has outgrown the old law, he cannot return to his childhood.

There is no God. The statement sounds discordant and unreal, even to ears which do little more than hear a word without meaning. Therefore, those who call themselves Christians must explain how it is that they can do so and still believe that God is no more.

II

The great discoveries of science, art, philosophy, and religion come quickly and without warning, surprising by their very simplicity. It seems to us nowadays merely a matter of common sense that the earth is a planet, a tiny fragment of a galaxy set in a multiplicity of galaxies; that matter itself cannot be analyzed to its smallest particle; that poetry need not alliterate or rhyme; that a true representation need not be photographic; that the interpretation of a painting lies as much with the onlooker as the artist; that our words and actions contribute to the roles we play throughout life; that we can never fully know our motives; that a criminal is a sick person; that "objective" arguments are projections of our own deepest knowledge and fears. These ideas, of course, are not held with equal confidence by everyone, but all of them qualify as reasonable to a modern ear. Yet each of them, in its day, was decried and attacked loudly as gross, heretical, inartistic, or barbarous.

The reason is not far to seek, though we evade its implications. An idea is widely held. It works. It meets the questions of the day satisfactorily. It is popular among the rulers of the community. It is built into law, religion, custom, morals, and language. One day a great man offers a simple question or statement which throws doubt upon our working idea. The new statement is reasonable, often more reasonable, than the old; but, for some reason as yet unexplained, an idea that has been held for centuries is considered better than one that is new. It is as though every year which passes gives added substance to a belief, independently of its truth. There is opposition to any new idea from those who are entrenched in the systems of law, religion, morals, customs, and even language. If the new idea is clear and provable, it is eventually taken up by the prophets, those who perceive the drift of events. At last it becomes accepted, analyzed, and itself built into law, religion, custom, morals, and language. Then, in due time, the whole extraordinary procedure starts all over again.

An obvious example was the idea that the sun moved round the earth. It was widely held. It worked. It met the questions of the day, explaining why night followed day which followed night. It was popular among the rulers of the Western World, giving the common people dimensions of security, inevitable law, and the fear of appearing to be an upstart. It became integral to the thinking of lawyers and religious leaders, and built itself into the language. When men talked about the sun rising and setting, they meant exactly and literally what the words said.

One day a simple question was asked, and history was never

the same again. Was it possible that the earth actually went round the sun? Opposition was overwhelming. The exponents of the new ideas were quickly discovered to be heretics, immoral, disloyal to the clear facts of God and nature. In due time, the idea's inherent merits led to its wide acceptance. And there the matter lies for the moment. During the few centuries which have elapsed, the belief has been extrapolated far beyond the knowledge or dreams of its original creators; but it has never been threatened by some simple brand-new question that runs counter to it. There may never be such a question. If there is, we may be sure that it will be opposed on many grounds, including, no doubt, the familiar one raised against Copernicus – that it upsets the people.

In the world of science, where there is some chance of agreement, the illustration is clear enough. How much clearer it is in the world of religion, where the agreed-upon facts are few! Here all the emotional resistance to change is reinforced. There being little data, faith can be held long beyond the point of reasonableness. Its basis being "relevation," it can be held, even when such facts as are available make it seem unlikely or impossible. The problem is compounded by the fact that, as new simple questions are asked in theology, they command less supportive data than new simple questions asked in science, with the result that opponents of theological change may operate more successfully than opponents of scientific change. Yet in spite of this (and on that account, perhaps more convincingly), change *does* take place, and the process outlined above is followed through, though at a more leisurely and hurtful pace.

There are many examples from the past. The Bible was written and edited like any other set of books. It is susceptible to the same type of analysis. Jesus did not claim to be God. The sacramental bread is not the flesh of Christ. We do not have to use certain forms of worship to please God. Jesus did not rise physically from the dead. The rituals prescribed in the Old Testament are not for all men throughout all time. The list could be expanded, almost without limit; and each statement would be one which, in its time, was strongly and vigorously opposed.

The simple question being asked today is: "Is God dead?" The answer, given in a variety of ways, is: "Yes."

The phrase "God is dead" is usually attributed to the German philosopher Friedrich Nietzsche, possibly the most misunderstood of all philosophers. It is not here, however, that we can trace the meaning that the phrase carries today. Nietzsche, though he clearly possessed a great admiration for Jesus (he exempted him, for example, from his accusation that Christianity is basically a religion of resentment), is more in the league of the old-fashioned atheist. When he says that "God is dead," he seems to be suggesting that *belief* in God has died. His own conviction seems to be that there is no God, and that there never has been.

In contrast to Nietzsche, it is fair to say that, though there may well be prototypes and forerunners, our present generation is the first to permit a man to state several things at once: I am a Christian; I follow Jesus; I belong to a certain long-lived denomination; and I do not believe in God. Werner Pelz, who entitled a book *God Is No More*, is a Church of England vicar; William H. Dubay, who asserts that Christ "did away with religion," is a Roman Catholic priest; John Robinson is a Church of England bishop; Father Jackson, who says, "If there is a God, we can't speak of him as a supreme being," is a university chaplain; Thomas Altizer, who wrote *The Gospel of Christian Atheism,* is an Associate Professor of Bible Studies at an American university; I am a Priest of the Anglican Church of Canada. I claim to be a Christian and an Anglican; yet I can say, in all seriousness, that there is no God.

At first sight, this makes nonsense. When the "God is dead" issue was raised in the Toronto *Telegram* of January 28, 1966, five people were asked: "Some people say 'God is dead'; what do you say?" They replied, in a variety of ways, "Of course not." Their explanations were reasonable, and would, in fact, be echoed by most people asked that particular question. For the old distinction is still assumed to be axiomatic: if you are a Christian, then you must believe in God; if you do not believe in God, then you must be an atheist, and a Christian cannot be an atheist. It is one of the discoveries of the present age that you can be both a Christian and an atheist.

What does it mean? When you try to find out what people mean when they say they do believe in God, you discover that there is little in common among the various answers. It is, therefore, no surprise to discover that there are as many varieties of Christian atheists as there are varieties of Christian theists.

IV

The first style of Christian atheism is probably the easiest for the traditional churchgoer to accept. The word "God" is a dangerous one. It means different things to different people and, whatever the careful theologian may think he has said, the meaning that comes through is that of a grand being who exists somewhere in space, who controls our lives, who helps us and punishes us, who intervenes in nature to perform miracles, and who needs to be constantly praised, pacified, flattered, and adored. If he is neglected, he becomes angry. It may well be, as has been suggested, that this is not a fair interpretation of the deities of the more sophisticated theologians such as E. L. Mascall; but it is the interpretation that has, through sermons, popular books, and radio, reached the general public. Recently, a group of women were discussing with Roman Catholic theologians certain doctrines that they found offensive. The theologians, in the face of some severe criticism about the negative, denigrating nature of Christian teaching, insisted that theology was concerned with "life" and always had been. "Then," came the reply, "you had better think again. What we have heard over the years is that you are obsessed with death." The criticism offered by the women was, in my opinion, correct. Whatever may have been the bead of hope in the minds of the thinkers and writers, traditional dogma came through as having a destructive and highly negative view of man. There was an obsession with death, punishment, and sinfulness.

The portrait offered by the Church in the past was one that

described God's love in terms that a merely average father could easily surpass. First, there was Heaven (restricted to the good), Purgatory (those on the way), and Hell (those who did not make it). All this provided a backdrop for the constant assertion that man was an unworthy being. Thanks to Christ, he might still be saved, but the gift was clearly a conditional one. He had to live a good life or, if he lived a bad one, he had to repent.

This attitude is still to be heard in a vast number of sermons in church and most of those on radio. I recently made an arbitrary analysis of some sermons preached in Toronto during four weeks. I telephoned twenty-five people who attended Church on those Sundays. I asked them: "Did the preacher seem to think that man is good or bad?" In eighteen cases, the replies were that the preacher did not think highly of man. The remaining seven had difficulty understanding the question. I then asked: "I mean – would you say your preacher thinks mankind is filled with goodness or filled with sin?" All replied that the preacher had suggested neither, but they thought the second was nearer the mark. Only one said that he thought his preacher felt that there was goodness in man. I asked him: "The average man?" The reply: "Oh no. Those saints." I asked: "Would you like to be a saint?" The reply: "What do you think?" and a laugh. Nobody thought that the Church's position was positive.

If one turns to the prayer book of the Anglican Church, any doubts about the attitude of traditional theology evaporate. The only good in the world is the good that God gives us to counteract the human bias towards evil; with which, to be specific, he is said to be born. I can find no example in the prayer book of a phrase which implies that God accepts us as we are; in other words, that he really loves us. The implication throughout is that love has to be earned; that God only accepts those who are prepared to surrender everything they are; and, even at the human level, this falls far short of love. From time to time, it looks as though we are about to be offered a genuine example of the unconditional offering of himself or the unconditional acceptance of us. Instead, there are always modifications. He pardons and absolves – all those who truly repent and unfeignedly believe his holy Gospel. Those who call themselves

Christians and obey the law of the Church, these alone seem to be granted acceptance. A poverty-stricken sort of love.

As I have said, it may be that the refinements of more subtle theologies have gone deeper than this and stated that God does in reality accept us as we are, whatever we are, without any conditions. But they have never communicated this, and even modern ones, like E. L. Mascall, aware of the modern pulse, still offer a chess game which is said to be the proof of God's being. The Mascall God is as loving as cold porridge.

In any case, it is this God who is now said to be dead; and such a death is greeted with pleasure by many who also claim to be traditional and orthodox Catholics. In effect, such men say: "When it is declared that God is dead, and it turns out that the God who was believed in was a terrifying, punishing, bearded monarch, then indeed he is dead. In really deep theology, he was never alive."

The first style of Christian atheism, therefore, causes very little trouble. The God in space; the God who punishes; the God who is tyrannical; the God who likes to see his children suffer if they are disobedient; the God who believes in prisons; the God who likes women to suffer in childbirth; the God who persecutes mankind because Eve ate an apple; this God is dead. About time, says one group. He never really lived, says another. If you would only do your homework better, you would know that theologians never taught such a God, says a third.

V

The second style of Christian atheism, also within the borders of traditional dogma, is evolutionary. God is eternal and unchangeable, but man consistently develops in his appreciation of the objective reality. The ideas of God, which were set out in the early books of the Old Testament, were developed in the later books, reached a high peak in the New Testament, and have been continually enlarged and refined ever since. It is taken for granted that ideas of God are always changing; that many of these ideas die and are replaced by better ones. Yet, through all the changes, we are only moving to a clearer vision of what is unchanging. We see through a glass darkly at best, but as the grime and dirt are wiped away, we see more sharply the God who ever was, still is, and ever will be. To him belong the glory and the motivation for seeking him; to him is always the initiative, to him the spring of love and activity and creation.

This style accepts that theological language needs constant reworking. Words come and go. They reflect the customs and thoughts of the age in which they are used. Metaphors have to be analyzed and, when they die, must either be replaced with new ones or their old significance made plain. Such words and metaphors are: redemption, atonement, sacrifice, ransom, blood sacrifice, suffering servant, saved, incarnation, resurrection, passion, gentile, samaritan. They have little or no meaning for modern readers. Let us, therefore, change them or explain them in new ways, so that new men may understand. All through this process, there is no thought that the underlying meaning has changed or could change. Find a new word, explain it in new ways: we are still redeemed, still in need of salvation, still saved through the blood of the lamb.

Many who hold to this style are willing to alter the word "God." They admit that it has little or no meaning for modern man. Having no meaning, let us put it on the shelf for a few years and find some way of talking Christianity without it; or keep the word and describe it in modern terms. This task was undertaken by such writers as C. S. Lewis, Dorothy L. Sayers, and J. B. Phillips. They took the word "God," which they conceded had become too small, and gave it strength and fullness. Under their skilful hands, the word regained some meaning and gave an impression of relevance to the lives of readers. Yet it was an old meaning that they were restoring. It did not occur to any of the above writers that God himself might change, or that he might have died. Such a suggestion would have been dismissed as altogether outside the range of the word. For them, God was alive as he had always been. Time had grown barnacles around the word and its meaning; they removed the barnacles .Time had watered down the reality; they restored it to full proof. Generations of misuse had distorted the basic elements of love and hope into caution and respectability; they took away the distortions. As a result, the word "God" was returned to circulation, renewed, and purified. These writers justly receive our praise and thanks.*

Lewis, Sayers, and Phillips served their turn and left a mark which will not disappear. Yet there was one weakness that they did not deserve to face: the appeal they made was to a declining number of people. To the majority, they conveyed little because even the purified, strengthened, and logically attractive God they described came through as irrelevant. Many of those who were interested also found these English thinkers a little too neat, as fool-proof as the mathematical and logical puzzles that were so popular in the thoughtful magazines of the day.

VI

The approach of Lewis, Sayers, and Phillips was, in fact, pushed aside by the work of men whom the three great restorers did not analyze; and it is these men who are now (often unrecognized by name) identified in the public mind with the new thinking among Christians. *The New Yorker* rightly selected the Bishop of Woolwich, Dr. John Robinson, as the key figure. Yet Robinson himself, though he is an original and creative theologian, made no claims to originality in his examination of the new ideas about God. He drew extensively from other men who had considered the same problem: Tillich, Bonhoeffer, Bultmann. Robinson's famous book *Honest to God* contains a higher proportion of lengthy and direct quotations than most popular theology.

It is not my purpose to do more than refer to the work of these men. In brief, Robinson set out a thesis which made an immediate appeal, not only to those who had detached themselves from modern denominational Church life, but to those who were caught up in it and wished to remain in it. Men used to believe in a three-decker universe, with Heaven above, the earth upon which they lived in the middle, and Hell beneath. God was

---

*It is worth noting that Dorothy L. Sayers was, in her day, violently attacked for her radical "blasphemy" in writing *The Man Born To Be King*, now a conservative classic.

thought of as "up there," the devil as "below." When the flat-earth philosophy came to an end, the God "up there" was replaced by the God "out there," and the devil remained below, in the middle of the earth, though he also walked on it. The change in metaphor caused few problems and, as time passed, the Biblical narratives, which presumed "up there," were read by men who assumed "out there," and no dissonance was felt. As the centuries moved on, the devil slipped away. Although he is recalled periodically when it is suggested that he be removed from the Church of England Catechism, little blood flows through his veins these days.

With new discoveries in modern astronomy, it eventually became difficult to retain even the metaphor "out there." When a Russian astronaut announced that he had seen no angels in space, he created very few problems for most present-day Christians, who had tacitly dropped the idea of angels in any case. Yet the astronaut's remarks caused some concern, not only for those who still carried on a belief in God in outer space, but also for those who did not. If God is neither "up there" nor "out there," then where is he? The question, which had been lying dormant, was now thrust upon us. The successors of Lewis, Sayers, and William Temple picked up the thought that God was a spirit and demonstrated that the old physical notions were crude, that they needed to go.*

Tillich and company, however, were pursuing other lines of thought and, though they are still not fully appreciated, they are finding their work widely accepted as valid. Paul Tillich expresses the popular viewpoint, though his view needs interpreting to many Christians who have for long been irritated with the God who stands outside them, behaving like a spoiled Oriental potentate. They have sat uneasily with the idea that God is somehow Other. It is true that the conception of the unlocated Other is more convincing than the God "out there," but only after a limited fashion. For Otherness is still, in a sense, out

_____

*As always, when a change in doctrine is made, some theologians insist that the departing idea was not really taught anyway. This sounds like Scrooge not only taking pleasure in his reform but insisting that he had never really been mean.

there. It is still someone greater and bigger and very authoritarian, Big Daddy, and kindly-allow-me-to-know-best. Otherness still comes over as the hidden, punishing God who will be angry if we do not grovel and say we are sorry. Like the God "up there," "out there," and "unseen yet ever present," this Other is, as Julian Huxley said, "Beginning to resemble not a ruler but the last fading smile of a cosmic Cheshire Cat."

Is the Cheshire Cat a reality at all? Viewed physically, all is gone; only the smile remains. Is this all we can say? Tillich thought not. Instead, he evaded altogether the search for the God above or beyond us and concentrated on what he called "the depths of our being." He said that God was the "very ground of our being." When we look at ourselves, we find that we are concerned about many things. God, said Tillich, is the ultimate among these concerns; he is our Ultimate Concern. Find out that which is our ultimate concern, answer its unconditional demands, and we have faith. It is an act of the whole personality. The word "God" is a word that represents our Ultimate Concern. There is nothing beyond it because then it would no longer be ultimate. We cannot fully understand it because then our understanding would be ultimate.

The appeal of Tillich's definition was immediate and is already commanding widespread acceptance. The old definitions of God had meshed with the lives of the people of those days – lives in which there was a hierarchical and ordered system, in which the king was more important than the peasant; the bishop more important than the curate; the giving of rules and the obeying of them the hallmarks of a civilized and religious community. The new definition offered by Tillich meshes with the lives of modern men. It speaks to a society in which men are coming alive and appreciating their full value. In this society, men are learning to be responsible to themselves and for themselves. They can blame nobody else for their problems; they can praise nobody else for their successes.

Let us examine the implications of this in a context much loved by the traditional theologian: that of the good and evil inherent in mankind. Modern man is, in a wide variety of research projects, examining the rise and fall of Hitler. He sees in the concentration camps of Auschwitz and Belsen the consequences of long years of Christian theology which assumed that God's logic was the logic of the monarchical law-court. The Jews had killed Christ and had accepted that his blood would be upon them and their children; Christ was God; therefore the Jews had killed God; therefore God's blood was upon them; therefore they must be punished forever; therefore it was right to punish them, and those who did so retained clear consciences. That Hitler's method was a mockery of Christ is obvious; that it made a mockery of Christian theology was not so obvious. For, though there had been untold compassion for the obedient, the Church had lit many bonfires around the human bodies of those who refused to conform, obey, and bow. The fires which burned John Huss, Joan of Arc, Thomas More, Bishop Cranmer, and the New England witches ultimately fired the ovens of Auschwitz and Belsen.

To the majority of people today, however, this apportioning of blame is irrelevant. In the person of Hitler may be seen the final blasphemy of the Catholic doctrine of punishment; but modern man cannot use the blasphemy to protect himself. He knows that there are many great crimes and cruelties in the world, and he can only blame man for them; he can accuse neither the old Church nor the devil. Auschwitz and Belsen were the products of men's minds. They were man's responsibility, and man, acknowledging this, must take to himself the task of moving beyond them into maturity. Nor need we remain in the past for our examples. In our own day, we are faced with Viet-Nam and the horrors of military control of outer space. These are, again, the creation of men's minds, and man alone can deal with them; there is no longer an appeal possible to the God "up there," "out there," or "beyond" us. The old God, who was supposed to love mankind and intervene on behalf of the weak, rarely did so and showed little concern except for the big battalions. Modern man knows that he is on his own. To him falls the full responsibility for his actions; and there is little evidence that he shows enough concern.

This, of course, is no counsel of despair. Like the traditional theologian, the new Christian is in a fix; like him, he can see the powerful presence of hope. The traditionalist, faced with undeniable evidence that God did almost nothing about cruelty, replied by setting the events in a wide context of God's eternal love and concern. Modern man, faced with undeniable evidence that he creates and perpetuates cruelty, sets the events in the wide context of man's positive drives towards truth, goodness, and beauty. In doing so, he seeks the positive road which he hopes will one day help him deal with the basic malaise which produced Hitler.

The traditionalist also notes that these strong moral values are deep-rooted in human nature and, recognizing that they are widespread, argues from them to the presence of God who has made them possible. Where do these values come from, he asks, and his answer is God. He then proceeds to set out the various deductions and applications which can be made from this. It is his privilege to do so; and nothing set down here must be construed as attacking it or reducing its value.

To fewer of us, however, does it make its old appeal. Instead of seeking the explanation of truth, goodness, and beauty in metaphysical terms, we prefer to examine them in a more pragmatic way by looking at tangible events in which people are *seen* to be helped. Modern man prefers to explain truth, goodness, and beauty, not by posing the existence of some Other Being, but by examining the evidence, primarily of medicine and science. This makes good sense to him because he perceives that cures in these areas far outnumber the miraculous cures of prayer, that they do so daily instead of spasmodically, and that they impose no conditions upon the patient beyond a willingness to be cured.

Above all, modern man is discovering himself. Psychology and psychiatry are daily opening new strait and narrow paths to the depths of man's being. As they are opened, there are fewer extravagant claims to solving all human problems; there is more caution; there is more honest declaration of uncertainty and ignorance. There is, at the same time, more that can be seen by everyone as true discovery. As man digs to deeper levels of his being, he becomes more certain that he will never be able to say, "I now know everything about myself, my neighbour, and mankind." He is in the realm of facts that are beyond his present comprehension. It is true that there are new and highly complex computers which will enable man to extend his brain as machines have extended his body. They will, if the military experts do not end humanity prematurely, lead to a new surge of evolution, which will change our present inadequacy. Though we can only prophesy in great ignorance and therefore in faith, it seems safe to say that, as this surge of evolution takes place, it will produce not a confidence that man will one day know himself completely but rather that he never will.

To live with uncertainty is to mature.

What, then, are we to do? It is tempting to say, "Perhaps we shall have to believe in God after all. He represents the eternal, that which is always beyond man's searching, that which is perfect and absolute in love, truth, and beauty; that which identifies the helplessness which man himself knows himself to be." In believing in God, however, we need not return to the traditional Other who is outside of us. Tillich has responded for many of us,* and it is as though we hear him saying: "Right. We do need God and we do need the word. I suggest that we seek its meaning in the depths of our being, which you have described, concentrating not on those things which are unknowable but on those which are clearly known. Then you feel certain that you are in search of God."

God is our ultimate concern, the ground of our being. Or you may prefer the statement made by a boy of ten when, cutting through a sermon in church, he asked the man in the pulpit: "You're really saying that God is a search, aren't you?"

VII

More recently, a new style of interpretation has entered the Christian Church. It seems slightly odd, almost kooky, and it still creates amusement in some circles. None the less, although

*Paul Tillich is a very complex and difficult writer. It is most unlikely that he would ever have employed such words as these. I am merely stating how I have heard him. If you wish to check your own reactions, examine his three volumes of *Systematic Theology* or his short, very condensed *Dynamics of Faith*.

I cannot yet fully understand it or share its convictions, I am convinced that this is a style of Christianity that will remain. It is highly creative, it meets certain facts more clearly than Tillich or Robinson do, and it opens up a whole new arena in which a Christian may truly live. Its exponents are manifold. The best known are probably Thomas Altizer and William Hamilton.

Their ideas are set out, especially in Altizer's writings, at a deep and refined level. There are, however, certain basic assumptions that all can grasp. The chief assumption made by Altizer and Hamilton is a simple one. There once was a God – now there is no God. He once lived but, somewhere in history, he died. At first sight, due to the brainwashing of Western schooling, this may seem nonsense. Our systems of education encourage us to believe in God; allow (sometimes grudgingly, as in England or Ontario) a plurality of beliefs about Him; and accept as logical, though ungentlemanly, the idea that he does not and never did exist. To say that there once was God but that he died, and that we can find out when he died, creates problems.

As Hamilton explains it, the new suggestion does not say that there never was a God; it does not say that man invented the idea of God to meet his purposes and that he no longer needs the notion; it does not say that there is a God whose description changes as man evolves. The new suggestion is categorical, real, definitive, and permanent. God once really lived; he no longer lives. He is dead, not because he never existed, nor because he was misunderstood into oblivion; but because, like a human being, he died.

When I first read Thomas Altizer's thesis in *The Gospel of Christian Atheism* (Philadelphia: Westminster Press, 1966), I found myself puzzled; and I still feel that he is offering as much a dogmatic act of faith as that of the traditional Catholic or the traditional atheist. It is highly metaphysical and, as in traditional theology, we constantly meet the word "must." Yet when I apply his thinking to another area of theological thought, I find that his theory is very suggestive. It makes sense of a problem which has nagged me for a quarter of a century: "Do angels exist?"

So far as early Christian and Jewish literature is concerned, they exist and are described with some precision. They form an innumerable multitude, beings intermediate between God and

50

man. In Isaiah and Job, they form a court to sing praises to God and to act as agents for him. Three of them are named: Michael, Gabriel, Raphael. The early New Testament accepts them as promulgators of the law. Jesus refers to them as spiritual beings who see God in Heaven and will be with him at his second coming. Angels appear at certain moments of Jesus' life: before his birth; in the desert when he is tempted; at his agony in the Garden of Gethsemane; at his Resurrection. The portrayal of angels reaches its climax in the Book of Revelation.

Angels, then, were thought to exist, and we note that when Gabriel appeared to Mary, though she was perturbed at his words, she accepted his presence. Angels were taken for granted, even by a simple middle-class girl. Somewhere in history, they disappeared. Descriptions of their appearance are few and those suspicious. Not even the theologians, who argue subtly about the various ranks of angels or their immaterial nature, mention that they have appeared within living memory. If a man today were to say that he had met an angel, he would quickly find himself on radio and television. Like flying saucers, they would be news; unlike flying saucers, they would not be taken seriously by anyone.

How can this discrepancy be explained? The obvious explanation is that there never have been angels. This seems to be the tacit assumption of most Protestant preachers and writers. We have then to explain the early descriptions in terms of imaginative recall or the vivid images of ecstasy. But ecstasy has not disappeared, and man's imagination is as vivid as ever. Another explanation is that they served their purpose and are no longer used by God in the way he formerly used them. This may be the Roman Catholic point of view. As with Protestants, Catholics pull away from too much speculation on the subject, but they do teach certain beliefs: that angels exist, that they are perfect in their spiritual lives, that they were created before man, and that they may be treated as the saints are treated. Unfortunately, nobody takes the trouble to describe any present-day appearances. Altizer's theories suggest another explanation. There were once angels, as described in the Bible, but they died. They have ceased to exist, in the same way that other parts of the created world have ceased to exist.

If God once lived, but has died, there is some need to answer the question, "When did it happen?" These are, of course, early days for full explanations. Altizer makes one very strong answer: the incarnation. The arrival of Jesus in the world made it clear that man no longer needed a heavenly God. God was now man, and there was no call to revert to a God who was Other than man. In order that he might become fully man, God gave up his "primordial and transcendent form" and became fully incarnate in the word or body of Jesus, and "thus he ceases to be present or real as the God who alone is God." In other words, God died in Jesus, who became, in William Blake's phrase, "The Universal Humanity." "Jesus," says Altizer, "is the name of the love of God, a love that eternally dies for man. Truly to pronounce his name — and for the radical Christian the names of Jesus and God are ultimately one — is to participate in God's death in Jesus and thereby to know the God who *is* Jesus as the expanding or forward-moving process who is becoming 'One Man.'" The radical Christian, in Altizer's theology:

> proclaims that God has actually died in Christ, that this death is both a historical and a cosmic event, and, as such, it is a final and irrevocable event, which cannot be reversed by a subsequent religious or cosmic movement. True, a religious reversal of the death of God has indeed occurred in history, is present in the religious expressions of Christianity, and is now receding into the mist of an archaic, if not soon to be forgotten, past. But such a religious reversal cannot annul the event of the death of God; it cannot recover the living God of the old covenant, nor can it reverse or bring to an end the progressive descent of Spirit into flesh.

Earlier in the chapter, I said that new ideas are normally simple and, because of their simplicity, they are widely opposed. They seem to contradict commonsense, nature, and all accepted ideas. This one of Altizer's certainly runs full into the face of our training, education, and the assumptions of society in general. It challenges the prejudices of both the religious person and the traditional atheist.

The suggestion made here is that we do not dismiss the idea out of hand. There is much to commend it. If you like hard reading, try Altizer's *The Gospel of Christian Atheism*. It is very well-written, expressing in full beauty the deep philosophy that Altizer has created. It holds together as a great poem and, when finished, you may feel that you have a glimmer of what he is reaching for. But for our purposes, I merely wish to set out the simple basic idea. The Church has taught in the past that God came down to earth and became a man, Jesus of Nazareth. This man was both human and divine. In due time, he returned to heaven. The early Church had great difficulty resolving the relationship of the human and divine in Jesus and never answered it satisfactorily. The result showed itself later, for the Church soon returned to a belief in a transcendent God – that is, a God who is above and beyond us. As Jesus was divine, he also took over the attributes of this transcendent God. Somehow the whole life of Jesus degenerated into a method by which God and man, formerly estranged, were now brought together. It was a method which still left God out in space, with man grovelling at his feet.

Altizer's simple idea, which will survive and grow, is that God and Man really did become one in Jesus. The barrier was broken completely by the achievement of a complete identity. In order that man should become fully himself, the transcendent God, who indeed existed in the days of the Old Covenant, died, and Jesus was born. Altizer does not claim that the incarnation was a single event in time. He says that it moves throughout time. Hamilton, picking up this idea, suggests that we can see God dying in the period between the French Revolution and the First World War. Today, he concludes, we can see clearly that God is dead. God was dying in the nineteenth century; he is dead in the twentieth. Perhaps the whole matter is summed up most neatly in a remark by a Roman Catholic, Father William H. Dubay, in *The Human Church*: "Yahweh [Jehovah] was the first atheist."

In discussing the evidence of God's death, William Hamilton – a more direct exponent than Thomas Altizer – mentions the many conversations he has had with the pastors of his Church. They say, over and over, "Everything we do in the life of the Church is exciting and makes sense, except for Worship." This is the experience of many, perhaps soon to be the majority, of priests in the Anglican Church and not a few in the Roman Catholic. Though they are not always willing to articulate the fact in unequivocal words, their actions are significant. They are excited in many parts of their parish work, they find little inspiration in Church Services. If they feel guilty about this, they sometimes pray harder. Often they sense that a refurbishing of the ritual and ceremonial will help restore life. They press strongly for radical revisions of the prayer book. They import dancers to dance the mass; singers to sing the mass. The Communion becomes a relaxed interchange between members of a congregation. In spite of this enthusiasm, there is no escaping the cold conclusion that it is sometimes misplaced. There is no way of restoring worship, as presently conceived, to life. Unless it becomes a mutual interchange between the members of a congregation, it is a drag.

In other words, the point at which the parish is normally at its deadest is the one point which demands a belief in the transcendent God. Nothing else in the parish demands as much. The work among the men and women, though paying lip service to God, need do no more. You do not have to believe in God in order to enjoy teas and sales; seek counselling from the clergy; sing in concerts and choirs; perform religious plays and pageants; play the organ; visit the sick; help the bishop run synod committees; study theology; and so on. The only activity which necessitates a belief in God is the Service in Church; and it is here that most people either declare themselves to be bored; or, while stating their shock at such a suggestion, demonstrate it by their physical and responsive stance while taking part.

VIII

There, at the moment, lies the range of choice for the modern Christian. What the next years will bring forth remains to be seen; for most of us the choice is already wide enough.

1. We may believe that there is a God, as that term was interpreted until a few years ago, that is, as a person Other than man, greater than man, who has no beginning and no end, who made the universe and all that is in it and still survives his Creation, guiding mankind and revealing himself.

2. We may believe that there is indeed a God, but that traditional theology has missed the boat in describing Him. One of our big tasks is to describe him more accurately, more relevantly, to modern man. It is, however, the same God who is implied in 1. The difference here is simply that the orthodox description is rejected.

3. We may believe that the word God has meaning, but that the traditional concept of the Other is not possible and perhaps never was. We seek descriptions in the depth of our being, our ultimate concern, in the realms of natural science and human relationships. Though this belief is very different from 1 and 2, it preserves some of the old fabric and enables new definitions of such words as faith and doubt.

4. We may believe that the God described by early theology was a God who did indeed exist, but that he no longer exists. He lived, but he is now dead. Traditional theology has done us a disservice in perpetuating the pretence that he is alive.

5. We may believe that there never was a God, that there is no God now, and that there never will be. This is the converse of the traditional belief at its most rigid. It is a dogmatic faith as complete as the old ones of the Middle Ages, for which it is often a mirror statement.

At what point in this list is it impossible or hypocritical to remain a member of a Church? At what point is it impossible or hypocritical to call oneself a Christian? The answer given here is that, though a question mark may well be placed over 5, all the above are possible to a Christian, and that it remains to be seen whether they are possible to members of such ancient denominations as the Roman Catholic, Anglican, Methodist, Congregational, or United. To remain a Christian, one has to be a follower of Christ, and one may be such a follower while accepting any of the above beliefs, perhaps including 5.

IX

So far as the Churches are concerned, the matter remains unresolved. At the moment, it is the view of many Church leaders that you have to accept "the faith." If this position is pressed hard, then they will eventually have to define very precisely what this compulsory faith is. So far they have not done so. References are made to "the accepted and agreed beliefs of God" which are necessary to be a Christian; but no evidence is offered as to what they are.

In a correspondence triggered by an article in the magazine *Resource*, a group of clergymen in New Brunswick complained bitterly on the grounds that the article was contrary to one of the Thirty-Nine Articles. Yet these Articles are no longer generally accepted and, for most of us, including many traditionalists, they are a quaint museum piece. The prayer book then? But the prayer book is a function of the Church's changing beliefs, not their creator or permanent identifier. Put simply, it is open to the Church to alter the prayer book at any time. There is ample evidence that the changes in the future will be far more extensive than those of the past. It may well be that future prayer books will reflect the choice implied above and will no longer require any one belief concerning God.

Are the theologians the men to decide? Eugene Fairweather, the leading ultra-conservative theologian of the Anglican Church of Canada, challenged me in a letter to the Toronto *Daily Star*.

> According to the Reverend Ernest Harrison, "the idea of God as an all-consoling, powerful tyrant is gone." If Mr. Harrison honestly supposes that these words express the Christian doctrine of God (which the Ten Theologians have just reaffirmed), then at least one thing is clear: he cannot be accused of deliberately rejecting the Christian conception of God, because he obviously does not understand it well enough to accept or reject it. Can he name a single Christian creed which contains the idea of "an all-consoling, powerful tyrant" or a reputable theologian who teaches it?

Leaving aside the implication that I am an ignorant dolt in theology, I was delighted with the letter, because it demonstrated an unexpected point of agreement: neither of us believes in an "all-consoling, powerful tyrant." The point of difference was simply whether other theologians (I had made no reference to creeds in this context) agreed or not. As this was a secondary issue, which could easily be resolved by the average reader in his sermon-listening or his twiddling of the radio dial on Sunday, I felt no qualms. The letter stood firm.

There are, of course, other theologians who *do* disagree with Professor Fairweather and myself. The outstanding example is Dr. Billy Graham, the American evangelist, another ultra-conservative theologian but one of a different stamp from Dr. Fairweather. Yet somehow I felt that Fairweather might not see Graham as "reputable." The minute such a word creeps in, one can see that the theologians can no longer be the arbiters; and a brief glance at their work soon demonstrates why. There is little agreement among them. To call upon the theologians as arbiters for our beliefs is to call upon men like Mascall, Robinson, Pike, Fairweather, Ramsay, Pelz, Lewis, Bultmann, Tillich, Temple, Altizer, to name but a provisional handful. If we do this, then we will find that we have at least four of the above choices available to us.

Perhaps we will have to turn to "reputable" theologians. But this is impossible because we then have to decide which are the "reputable" ones, and who is to say? The Primate of Canada, one of the most charitable of modern Christian thinkers, referred recently to the need for sound theology. When challenged for information as to what constituted sound theology, he conceded that this was a task beyond him. Beyond him, as a modest thinker; he might have replied, with complete accuracy, beyond anyone.

Should we turn to the House of Bishops, as was suggested by Arnold Edinborough in *The Canadian Churchman*? The question need only be asked to be answered. Once again, the spectrum offered by bishops covers a wide range and, if we are allowed to associate ourselves with Ramsay, Robinson, Pike, Coleman (formerly of Kootenay) and Snell (of Toronto), then we again have the same four choices. Suppose the bishops were to agree on a doctrine of the Church which must be accepted on pain of excommunication? That question may be dealt with when the bishops completely agree. If they do, and it is accepted that their opinion is valid and binding upon all Church members (no easy task), then the choice may be limited. At the moment, there is no such clearly accepted statement.

Then where can we turn? The answer is, as it always was, that we have to decide for ourselves. If theologians, bishops, and synods provide no clear yardsticks by which to measure our membership, neither do the local clergyman, the assembled deaneries, or the congregations. This is no matter of a simple majority vote because, if a congregational majority turned out to support atheism, 5 above, it is very doubtful whether the rest would accept it, or should accept it. And what is sauce for the goose is sauce for the gander.

The choice, then, is for the individual, and for many of us it has already been made. We enjoy being members of the Church. It is here that we meet so many of the people we love. It is here that we are received as ourselves and can receive others in like fashion. We like the rector or the curate; we enjoy singing in the choir; we enjoy playing organs, drums, or saxophones. It is here that coffee houses are organized, meetings held which give us enjoyment. It is here that our children seem to have their good times. The teaching handed out in Sunday School may range from inoffensive to wretched; but it tries to impart good standards of behaviour; the children like the teacher in spite of the teaching. We may even have shopped around to see if there are any other groups that might provide the sense of belonging we need. The agnostics sound great on radio and television, but it is difficult to find out where they meet, and we like to meet people. The Unitarians sound as if they are on the right track, but there is an assumed intellectualism which may be bothersome, and their groups form something of a pattern. We occasionally have resurgences of the old convictions, occasionally feel that the old moralities had their point; and this make us embarrassed in Unitarian company. This is probably an unfair assessment of Unitarians, but events so stand for many of us.

In the absence of other groups which can receive us, and in the presence of the group which does receive us, we wish to remain members of our Church. If the traditional creedal follower wishes to sit down at coffee with us, we will be overjoyed; and very happy to listen to him. Let him tell us what he thinks the Gospel is, and if he genuinely believes it, let us raise flags of delight. Then let us tell him what we think the Gospel is and let him listen. If he tells us that he finds our beliefs different from his and that we must therefore get out of the Church, we must respectfully decline. We shall remain as long as we remain; and neither bishop nor priest, bell, book, or candle shall have any effect.

Here is some advice, therefore, for those who do not believe in God and are being told by clergy or fellow adherents that they cannot consider themselves loyal members: remain, so long as you feel that it is right for you to do so. If the Church demands a specific belief in a specific God, it must say so more clearly than it does at the moment. As things stand, your beliefs may well be orthodox in twenty years' time, and you may then be faced with the task of showing charity to those who are challenging them.

CHAPTER IV

Did Jesus Believe in God?

I

As soon as the Christian knows that the supernatural God is dead, he is liberated to walk into the presence of Jesus Christ. In our everyday existence, we must feel free if we are to know another person intimately. If I fear you, if I have some notion that you are above me, below me, or beyond me, then I am inhibited. In order to know you, I have to trust you completely. I must be certain of your love, whatever the circumstances.

As long as we believed in a transcendent God, we were inhibited from knowing Christ. As we moved into his presence, we were uncertain. We had to remember too many things: on the one hand, his divinity, his perfection; on the other, our unworthiness. A good illustration of the difficulties encountered if we tried to approach Jesus naturally occurred a few years ago when a girl in her late teens attended a class for Sunday School teachers. She was the only young person present. Much of the general chat of the evening revolved round the dreadful lives lived by young people today, the sad decay of contemporary morals, and the hope that the day would return when the rules and laws of the Church would once more be obeyed. The girl took this for a while and then began to point out some other factors. "When I go out at night," she said, "it's not the teenagers I'm scared of; it's the men your age. I think teenagers live their lives as well as they can." She was offered, by way of reply, the example of Jesus who would condemn the way of life lived by so many modern young people. She became annoyed and said: "Well, all I can say is I believe Jesus went through every sin in the book. He's just too human to put up with the stuff I've heard tonight."

There was an immediate uproar, and words like "irreverence" were tossed about. Such a reaction comes whenever, in an ecclesiastical gathering, a statement is made about Jesus that clashes with certain doctrines concerning him. Among traditional Christians, there is a complete absence of freedom in the presence of Christ. Did he have sexual intercourse with women? Did he ever boast? Did he make a mistake in accepting Peter's confession? Did he hate his mother? Was he hostile to his disciples as well as to the leaders of society? It is not that such questions may be answered one way or the other; in everyday Church circles, they are not allowed to be asked. The very questions are heretical.*

Once we are delivered from the ogre of the transcendental being who sees everything and forgets nothing, then we can greet Jesus as we greet the real friends of our life: in complete frankness, without hesitancy, with mutual joy, without striving, without grovelling, without delusions, with easy understanding that, whatever we say or do or think, it will be interpreted in our favour, and that whatever he does or says or thinks will be interpreted in his. Even the smallest elements of fear, duty, or self-negation will hurt the love we give and take. A belief in the transcendental God makes love impossible. That is why traditional theologians have spent so much time proving that love is, in fact, more subtle than simply the accepting of others and ourselves as we are, without strings attached, and why they seem to be more interested in discipline, law, and obedience. That love, if it is freely given, contains its own discipline, law, and obedience, is a clear fact to anyone who has loved. But these are created within the framework of the loving act; the standards are discovered within the situation. The minute they are imposed

---

* At a Council of Churches Conference on Family Life held in 1966, the following question was suggested as a good one to ask oneself: "When the woman wiped Jesus' feet with her hair, she performed a highly sexual action. Did Jesus at that moment experience sexual excitement?"

arbitrarily from outside or above us, then our inhibitions make it impossible for us to discover and identify them.

We can see, immediately, that friendship with Christ is impossible if we think of him as an eternal cosmic Word. Again and again we have turned Jesus into the old God – he who always was, who was self-created, who is, who always will be, who cannot die. Whatever was predicted of the God who lived under the Old Covenant is said to apply to Jesus of Nazareth who possesses all the attributes of Divinity. This puts him immediately outside the range of friendship. It is not possible to be friends with such a being who is by definition better, purer, and more refined. As we know in all the vibrant moments of our lives, friendship is based on what we have in common and is only possible if the gap between the life-standards of two people is bridgeable. The gap between the Divine Jesus and myself is not bridgeable, except on the sole initiative of the other person in the situation. So, runs the traditional teaching, the transcendent Risen and Ascended Christ stretches out his arms to bridge the gap. God and man become one again, and there is an atonement which restores the gap created by Adam's sin. A gap is bridged, however, only when there is an identity between the two people involved. It is impossible to maintain a friendship if one side is the giver, the other the receiver; if one side offers and the other takes part only by responding. In friendship, both parties have to give, both parties receive. If Jesus does not need me, then I may bow my knee and praise and glorify, but we will never be friends. Whatever the disparity between the characters of two friends, their relationship is based on an equality.

That there might have been such an equality – that, in fact, such an equality was implicit in the New Testament story – may be shown. The fact that Mother Church prevented the equality being seen and rejoiced in becomes obvious when we look at the expressions of her teaching in stained-glass windows and religious art in general. Here we meet Christ the King, Christ Risen to the Right Hand of God, Christ in Judgment, Christ Rewarding his Faithful, Christ Holding a Sheep in his Arms. Even the pictures of Christ washing his disciples' feet, one of the most significant events in his life, is portrayed as the Great Man humbling himself for a moment. The humility described carries a capital H; it is the Humility of the king who deigns to walk among his people, not the humility of the bum who asks for a handout. The Biblical story tells of events that show an equal relation between Christ and his friends; but it is soon drowned in the clamour that proclaims Christ as supreme. The Christ who is divine, the Christ of the creeds, and the Christ of the present prayer-book services is a Christ who eludes friendship.

II

In an attempt to escape this, many Christians sought, instead, the Jesus of History. These attempts are brilliantly summarized, though not approved, in Albert Schweitzer's *The Quest of the Historical Jesus*. In general terms, the scholars involved were trying to answer the question, "What was Jesus *really* like?" They took it for granted that the Church had given us a distorted picture, and they attempted to find the original. Great work was achieved, though it was not always popular, and some of the scholars found themselves dismissed from their teaching posts. The process was rather like that following the Second World War, when some of the old masters hanging in the British art galleries were cleaned. Over the centuries, the originals had been covered with layer upon layer of varnish, so that the pictures that the artists had painted could no longer be seen. The experts, knowing that the masters really knew how to paint, and that the dull miseries that were displayed in the art galleries were ridiculous, decided to remove the varnish and let the public see the real pictures. The work was done, but the public was far from happy, as angry letters to the newspapers soon demonstrated. For they had come to love the varnish. The old masters (assumed to be "great" because – well, because they were "great") were perceived only as they had been presented by the art galleries. When some viewers saw the familiar paintings in their original state for the first time, they were horrified. Was this what they had been taught to respect in their childhood? It was not, of course, and they rejected the cleaning as abhorrent and irreverent. The work continued; its pace was slowed.

Some Christians noted that the same thing had happened to the portrait of Christ. Mother Church had not only covered it with varnish but superimposed new pictures upon it, ranging from a king with a crown on his head to an anaemic butterfly. They decided to scrub the portrait clean, and they did a good job. Picture after picture was removed, layer after layer of varnish disappeared. The Christian public did not like it; the authorities liked it still less. Along with "the Social Gospel," the phrase "Historical Jesus" became a term of amused contempt in traditional circles. Fortunately, the scholars who wished to see Jesus as he was continued their work and have probably gone as far as they can go. Unfortunately, Jesus was not and is not a picture; and, though we have freed ourselves of nonsense, though we can perceive some of the historical Jesus hidden by the centuries of theological dogmatism, the portrait is obscure.

There are two reasons for this obscurity. The first difficulty is that it is never possible to reconstruct history in the same way that we can construct our lives. As we live, we receive signals constantly from all quarters, from friends, from news media, from within ourselves. We sense the atmosphere in which we live. Reconstructing this atmosphere is possible only by reliving it. This is historically impossible. All that remains of the past is the biassed and incomplete records of men who wrote as accurately as they could. We do not really know what Elizabeth I was like, or George Washington, or Wilfrid Laurier. A history book, no matter how long or well-written, can give only one man's interpretation of the documents that he has read, documents that often come from other documents, themselves human interpretations of the events of the day. The study of history actually does remove many layers of varnish and uncover many beautiful realities of the past. But a complete portrait eludes us, even if we have film, tape, and print to work with. History involves selection; the minute we select, we interpret. The portrait of Christ, without benefit of film, tape, or print, is even more selective. Scholars and historians like David Friedrich Strauss and Ernest Renan come up with a more convincing portrait of Christ than the traditional one, and a portrait closer to life than that of Mother Church, but it is still a picture and not a reality.

There is a second reason why the Historical Jesus will always elude us. Suppose that a full and true portrait of Jesus of Nazareth resulted from our labours. It would still be impossible to relate the portrait to friendship or love. You cannot love a portrait of a person who lived a long time ago; still less can you love an event or a process.* Thomas Altizer wrote about this:

> It is no less true that to identify Jesus wholly with a particular and isolated person or event of the past is to foreclose the possibility of his present life or forward movement. Indeed, we can know Jesus as the ancient Jesus of Nazareth only insofar as we are closed to his contemporary presence. Not only is this ancient Jesus alien and lifeless, but precisely for this reason he can be manifest in a religious form only as an abstract and distant Word or as an epiphany of a primordial Innocence. In either case we find a reversal of concrete experience, a flight from the actuality of consciousness and the body, a regression to a primordial moment of time. The uniquely Christian Jesus is the Jesus who is fully manifest in a present and actual moment of time.

III

The decision, then, that the Christian makes is whether to lose Jesus in the past or find him in the present. With no transcendent God breathing down his neck, he can think of Christ and be open to full friendship with him. He knows himself to be in a relationship with Jesus, a relationship of love. "I will call you friends," said Jesus to his disciples; if we are disciples, we will know ourselves to be his friends. This means that we enter his presence on the only basis known to friendship, mutual acceptance, and an equality of bearing.

In doing this, we necessarily meet ourselves. In all the deep-ranging, immediate events of our lives, we discover ourselves. In our dreams, our waking events, our decisions, our sense of belonging, our anxiety, our fear, we become ourselves and see

---

*An old detective story, which became the movie *Laura*, begins with a chilling event in which a man falls in love with a portrait of a beautiful woman who is dead. She later turns out to be alive, but this spoils the story.

ourselves. My friend is my friend because he is also me, because I am him. Jesus is a friend to the extent that he is me and I am him. A scholar, poking fun at some theological opponents, described a Liberal Protestant as one who seeks Christ by looking down a deep, dark well and seeing his own reflection. In his anxiety to score a few points, he missed the significance of what he was saying. For, if I look into the face of a friend, I do indeed see myself; and this is the hallmark of all close friendship. For he also, looking into my face, sees himself. We are therefore one: I in him and he in me.

In this reciprocal relationship we can hear echoes of the Gospel according to St. John, and this raises the question: How do we know this Jesus? We know him in the present, the here and now, or we do not know him at all. We have his words. Spoken to other men, they speak to us, if we have ears to hear. They are not in the past, they are not limited to us. If we are warmed by their friendship, we respond and are Christian.

Perhaps the most creative effort to undertake this act of friendship resulted in Werner and Lotte Pelz's book *God Is No More.* The title was borrowed from a line in William Blake's long poem *The Everlasting Gospel*: "Thou art a Man, God is no more." Acknowledging that "awkward and pious hands have from the beginning interfered with those sayings and have sometimes succeeded in twisting them almost beyond recognition," they insist that "in most instances the imaginative ear can still pick out the sound of an intensely personal, hopeful, and human voice. . . . The problem of authenticity is ultimately not a scholar's problem, since it is not a question of authorship but of relevance – just as the ultimate justification of the *Iliad* does not lie in its Homeric parentage but in its beauty."

Whenever I read the Pelzes' moving response to Jesus' offer of friendship, I am slightly jealous and yet slightly encouraged. Their response is certainly not my own, and it might not be yours. The friendship Jesus offers Werner and Lotte Pelz is a very middle-class one, a friendship of good music (they do not hear the beauty of the hit parade), of good art (no weekend comics), and good writing (Shakespeare, not Ian Fleming). It is a friendship that is always delicate, always fragile, offering promises of a wholeness always in good taste, conjuring up images of good food well cooked, served with the right wine. I am jealous because they have his friendship in a way that I cannot have, and yet that I recognize as true. Jesus is like that. He gives himself like that, and he receives back the Pelzes as they are. They look into his face and they see themselves.

So I read the words for myself and something happens within me that might make the Pelzes jealous too. Unlike them, I love the city, the machines, the gadgets, the statistics that they see as different from the problems of birth and death, love and friendship. I do not make their distinctions, and I do not think that, in loving these glorious tributes to man's ingenuity and the means of full living, that I have "bent the knee to Baal." Jesus comes to me as I am. I notice that he used the gadgets of his day, the products of carpenters' shops. He took advantage of people's hospitality, fed upon their food, went fishing, walked and breathed the air, rode the best vehicle he could achieve, lived it up among drunkards, and maybe got drunk. He complained about the luxury of the rich, not because it was comfortable but because they denied it to other people.

In the interchange between Jesus and ourselves, whoever we are, we find relationships that flow two ways. The Pelzes do not come before him grovelling or bullying, but in order to share equally, face to face. They do not seek a Divinity above and beyond men, which deigns to condescend for a moment in time. They know him as he knows them.

IV

It is as though Jesus is saying to those who listen: "Why do you call me God?" He is irritated because we keep eluding him as he is and keep seeking some far-off perfect being. His questions challenge us to feel more deeply, to look into ourselves more deeply. He is a man, living his life to the full, pulling back from nothing, whether it gives exquisite pleasure or leads to death. He is, surely, God. "What more do you want?" he seems to be saying. "The God, who inhabits eternity, is no more; he no longer dwells in the vast untapped spaces; he no longer sits upon a throne; he no longer intervenes in history to win a war or punish a king. He is here, a man, among you. I am God," he concludes, and waits for the true response of friends.

It is impossible, trying to push through the mass of words which fills the past two thousand years, to know exactly what was originally said. It is impossible to know whether any of his hearers were able to make the response of friends and say, "We, too, are God. We are your friends. In you, we see ourselves. In us, you see yourself. We, too, are God."

Jesus rarely spoke of God; he spoke more often of the Father. When he used the word God, it was most typically when he spoke of the Kingdom of God. It was this which he offered, this which he urged his followers to enter. Installing his Kingdom, he struck a new note, unheard before. No longer was the Kingdom that of a great monarch set on high above men; no longer was the God the transcendent eternal being. The King and the God were, Jesus said, already present, already among men; the Kingdom was already established. It was not perfect. It was, he said, even among the Pharisees. It was a very earthy kingdom, among men, part of their day-to-day lives. No power, no pack-drill.

Nor were there any dignities. As there was no powerful monarch, so there were no minions to serve and hold little powers of their own. James and John did not understand. They sought positions of honour in the Kingdom. Jesus snapped back that these were not possible. Positions he could not promise; they had missed the whole point. They saw the Kingdom as a hierarchy, with rulers and priests at the top and the people, obedient, at the bottom. Jesus would have none of this. He was equal with them. There were no rulers and no ruled in the Kingdom.

Time after time, men pursued Jesus for definitions and statements of faith; and he eluded them. Martha tried to pin him down that Lazarus would rise on the last day. The resurrection, replied Jesus, is here and now. "I am the resurrection and I am life. Nobody who is alive and has faith shall ever die. Do you believe this?" She did not hear what he was saying and made a mental obeisance to the Messiah. She did not perceive that he had offered her the sharing of a true friend, that she too was the resurrection and she too was life.

On the cross, driven by a terrible agony of separation, he cried out that God had forsaken him. The last link was broken. The union was to be renewed but, throughout the ages, there were always those who knew that Christ had died because he strove against the "wheel of religion" and cried out for men to be free of their rulers, their driving guilt, and their tyrant God. Jesus, like Yahweh, is the great Atheist.

V

Jesus rarely taught about God. Granted his upbringing in the particular age in which he lived, he would not be free of a belief in a deity. In the synagogue, the temple, on the streets, and in the fields, it was assumed that there was a God up there who controlled the destinies of the Jewish people. Naturally he could not throw away such a heritage, nor did he. When little hinged upon it, he raised no unnecessary question. But, when there was a clash, he trod the new road, away from God and his old law. At a dramatic, challenging level, he broke the sabbath; disrupted a synagogue service; viciously and unfairly attacked the religious leaders for their orthodox doctrines concerning prayer, sacrifice, and tithing; refused to concede the ritual food customs; and fulfilled the commandments by undercutting them at their weakest points.

He learned in the same way he lived. One of the most vivid stories in the New Testament tells of his encounter with a Phoenician woman. He had gone down into the territory of Tyre in order to take a rest. He found somewhere to stay and hoped that he would not be recognized. Like most doctors on holiday, he did not succeed. A woman came to him to cure her daughter of what seems today to be a psychological disturbance. She was (and this is important) a foreigner. Her religion was from the wrong side of the tracks; so was her nationality – she was a "Gentile." Jesus was tired, of course, but his reply came not merely from his fatigue but from the religious prejudice in which he had been reared. "Let the children be satisfied first," he snapped. "It is not fair to take the children's bread and throw it to dogs." A cruel remark, but one that flowed naturally from the orthodox view of his people. To the well-taught Jew, the cruelty would not be noticed, for was it not true that these other nations were god-killers? The irony here is immediately obvious – how soon Christendom was to switch the roles! The woman was not to be put off. She was not a Jew. She was not reared in his creed. She did not think that God was thus and thus. She may not have even believed in him at all. She therefore had no time for his argument. Driven by the need to have her daughter healed, she had the courage to say so. "Sir," she snapped back. "Even the dogs under the table eat the children's scraps." We have only to identify with her for half a second to realize that she was *not* saying, "I am a humble creature, O Lord, but surely, as the dogs eat the crumbs under the rich man's table, you will grant me my humble request." What she was doing was calling his error in the best possible way. Of all people, he was the angriest with those who said they were better than others. In her sensitive frame of emotions, she responded where it hurt him the most.

He immediately recognized his prejudice and the absurdity of what he had said. Like all good teachers, he was willing to learn and to acknowledge that, in learning, he had changed. "You're right," he says. "Off you go. Be content. Your daughter is better." She now knows him. She has given herself, and he has given himself. She has looked into his face and seen herself. He has looked into hers and seen himself. They have shared a mutual hostility; they are friends; they are one. They have both changed. She knows herself to be a full human being – not a mere woman, a mere Gentile, or a mere foreigner. She returned home to find her daughter well. The daughter was faced with a mother who knew that she was whole, who had discovered herself: the neurotic ailments had disappeared. The demon, or whatever it was, had departed.

I have built my interpretation into the retelling. This is my response. It may, or may not, be yours. Yet we may all ask a pertinent question. In a brilliant magazine article in *Resource* (January 1966), Catherine Gallup asked: "Was Jesus Prejudiced?" and used the above story to suggest that he was. A group of junior-high children, asked the question, replied, "No." They were then handed a mimeographed copy of the story, using the words of the New English translation. After a lengthy discussion, they decided that he had, indeed, been prejudiced against the woman, but had learned from it.

VI

He learned many other things as he moved through the years. As he talked, the old beliefs in God became very pale. He rarely talked about God and resisted all but the most ambiguous of descriptions. Instead, he talked of "The Father." What is he saying to us? We can only meet God in personal terms. "God is a spirit" relieves us of the notion that he is a giant king on a throne. But a spirit may simply circulate everywhere, be present everywhere, still somehow apart from and above mankind. A Father is a person in a personal relationship. It is a good metaphor because it is one that changes as the ages change. In an age when the Father was in strict charge of his family, to dictate and rule, men could perceive God in this way. In an age when a Father is on an equal basis with his wife and family, then we have a different perception. It has taken us two thousand years to reach this point, and there are signs that some people, not liking the freedom that an equal family involves, hanker for a return to the old, authoritarian father. They hanker in vain. The new family is different, not better in everything but more adept at that equal interchange between people, which love insists upon. Father may, indeed, take a lead in many things, as may Mother, as may the children. Leadership moves from one to the other. Nothing can be accepted any longer merely because "Father says so."

Put another way, Jesus preferred the word "Father" to "God." The latter signified too much the unchanging authority who was self-created and who could never die. The former offered a word whose meaning could change and grow. The word "God" is static; the word "Father" is mobile. The word "God" implies eternity; the word "Father" implies death. The word "God" admits of no equality; the word "Father" assures it. The word "God" is sexless; the word "Father" is sexful. The word "God"

71

is supernatural; the word "Father" is human. The word "God" is isolated; the word "Father" implies a relationship.

VII

Did Jesus believe in God? Who can say? There is the language that is retained long after the belief has evaporated. There is the need to evade as many theological discourses as possible in order to heal. There is the intrusive editing of the religious men who wrote the story down and injected their own moralizing about it. It may be that Jesus' belief in God was as deep and unquestioning as that of the mediaeval Catholic. It may be that, if challenged and willing to respond, he would have described God as Tillich describes him. He might even have responded as Altizer and asked: "Why do you keep on talking about God? You have me."

We need not, however, give up too soon. There is one detail in Paul Tillich's description of God which, in fact, fits all descriptions. That detail is the widely quoted statement that God is our "ultimate concern." If you can discover a man's ultimate concern, then you have discovered his God. This applies to the traditionalist as much as to the radical. How do we discover a man's ultimate concern? Jesus said that we should know men by what they produce. "If," wrote St. John, "a man says 'I love God' while hating his brother, he is a liar." We move, therefore, from Jesus' words to his actions. We are faced with the same difficulty as with the words – the alterations imposed by awkward and pious hands. Yet, in spite of the desire to smooth off and make things religious, the facts speak for themselves, enough of them at any rate to make us ask: "What was Jesus' ultimate concern?"

As soon as the question is asked, we are in the presence once more of a relationship between friends. We observe and we respond. Every man's response will be different; no man's less worthy or more worthy than another's. I respond to my friend's action in one way, you respond in another. He responds to our actions in different ways. There are no formulae for the appreciation of men's actions; and there is no formula for understanding those of Jesus Christ. If, then, the traditional Christian responds by seeing Jesus' ultimate concern as God Almighty, the mainspring of every charitable action, the cause of all his work, and the inspiration needed to perform it, then that is how he responds.

Today there are Christians who respond differently. They see Jesus' ultimate concern as the healing of people; the bringing together of those who are estranged; the tying up of the broken-hearted; the delivery of confidence to the poor; the raising of women to equal dignity with men; the righting of injustice; the overthrow of authority. It was not always so. On one occasion, faced with the clamour to heal the sick and preach to them, he withdrew into the wilderness and prayed. A pity, though he knew his own strength and must have been exhausted beyond measure. For the rest, his drive is in the direction of healing other human beings, not lecturing about God. At a deeper level, we find that he is concerned more with the healing than the presence of God in it. When a patient is ill, and God is relevant to his situation, then Jesus will commend him in these terms. When God's presence is not relevant, he makes no mention. Occasionally, he refers to the faith of the healed, though not always as faith in God. Often he makes no reference to faith at all. He does not use belief in God as a preliminary test. He neither gives nor withholds on the basis of an abstract dogma.

Examining what he did, how may we suppose that Jesus thought about God? As a judge? He condemned the judging of people. As a monarch? He was vitriolic in his denunciation of rulers. As a high priest? He condemned all priestly practices. As a person who exists above and beyond mankind? He gave scant attention even to the possibility.

For many of us, his ultimate concern was the close relationship he held with his fellow men. He talked to them in agreement, in affection, and in hostility. He made no pretence to getting along with his mother, yet he thought of her on the cross; he walked out on his family more than once, yet his brother was a leading disciple after his death. It is contrary to the majority teaching of the past, but it may be true to say that whatever Jesus believed about God was a consequence of his desire to be close to men so that they could truly become themselves. His love for

73

them did not derive from any love of a greater person known as God; love for his friends was his ultimate concern.

Who was Jesus? The question defies an answer. Who is he? We can only respond. If we respond by dismissing him as unimportant or irrelevant, then we are obviously not Christians. But, if we take him seriously, we may stand up and be counted. Taking him seriously does not mean that we have to take him in the manner of previous generations, nor in the way our religious leaders would have us do today. If you see him as God, then that is how you see him. If you see him as a man who was fully a man, then that is how you see him. Words like "orthodox" and "heretic" have no meaning in this context, any more than they do when I try to describe the love between myself and another. I love, therefore I love. It is no use telling me that my articulation of that love is "heretical," because "love" and "heresy" are words which never meet.

To say that you are a Christian means that you are in a living relationship with Jesus Christ. How you proceed to describe this is for you alone to decide.

CHAPTER V

Did Jesus Rise from the Dead?

I

The new Christian is called upon to face a living relationship with Jesus Christ, and he does so in terms of resurrection. One of the questions I find myself being most frequently asked when I speak on the subject of our new-found freedoms in today's Church is: "What about the resurrection? How do you explain that?" It is a good question, and some sort of a response is needed.

Two issues have to be faced. What are the events of the resurrection? In what way do we interpret those events? It need scarcely be said at this point that the conclusions of past generations of Christians form part of our study but carry no infallible authority. We have the responsibility to interpret the events for ourselves.

According to the Bible, Jesus' body was wrapped in the winding sheets of death and placed in a tomb. On the third day, the tomb is empty and he is risen. There are, of course, many discrepancies in the narratives as recorded in the four Gospels. The women who are to visit the tomb buy their spices and perfume on Friday, according to Luke; on Saturday evening, according to Mark.* The women who visit the tomb are described differently, as is the whole episode. In Matthew, two women – the two Marys

---

*The ending of St. Mark's Gospel (particularly from Verse 9 to the end) does not form part of earliest manuscripts and may not have been part of the original. This does not affect the discussion, of course.

— come; there is a violent earthquake; an angel descends from heaven, rolls the stone back, and sits on it; there are guards who shiver with fear; the angels tell the women what to do. In Mark, three women — the two Marys and Salome — bring the oils, see the tomb empty, and enter to find a youth wearing a white robe sitting on the right side; he tells them what to do. In Luke, three women — the two Marys and Joanna — bring the spices, find the stone rolled away from the tomb, and enter to find two men in dazzling garments at their side who tell them what to do. In John, the embalming is not done by the women at all, but by two men — Joseph and Nicodemus. One woman — Mary of Magdala — comes, finds the stone rolled back, and runs to tell the disciples, although she does imply later that she had companions. In Matthew, the women run off to tell the disciples and are met by Jesus on the way. In Mark, they say nothing to anybody, though they later "delivered all these instructions" briefly to "Peter and his companions." In Luke, the women report what they have seen to the eleven apostles and all the others. In John, Mary only reports the incident to Peter and John.

There are other discrepancies. Matthew and Luke appear to refer to the resurrection appearances as occupying a single day; John gives an account that spreads them over more than eight days; Acts fixes the period at forty days. But these are sufficient to show that, as the conservative theologian E. G. Selwyn put it: "The reconstruction of the scene at the tomb is far from easy, and it was probably no more easy for those who first tried to record it than for ourselves."

Why, then, did they record it? And why the description of an empty tomb? We can only guess, but there is perhaps a significant hint in St. Matthew's Gospel. He tells us that there was a story circulated that Jesus' disciples had stolen the body. It does not seem a very intelligent way of attacking the Christians, but, as Helen Milton says, "This doesn't mean that the story wasn't circulated. People in any generation may be found using futile and absurd methods to try to back up their convictions and positions." If this story was circulated, it is not farfetched to suppose that the Christians replied with a counter-propaganda story, that of the empty tomb. "Your disciples," say the attackers, "stole the body." "You're wrong," comes the reply. "The tomb was empty because an angel pushed the stone back." Because there is propaganda at work, the details become muddled, and where if the matter were historical we would expect very careful accuracy, we have events that cannot be reconciled.

It does not matter a great deal whether the story of the tomb arose as counter-propaganda in the way suggested, because these resurrection stories need not be taken as factual in any case. There may, therefore, have been other reasons why they were invented. Those reasons, however, were unlikely to be connected with any "proof" of Jesus' resurrection. It is, as a result, no surprise that St. Paul, though anxious to establish Jesus' resurrection, because it was essential to his teaching, did not mention the empty tomb. It would not occur to him to do so. It is only later, when the narratives had gathered around them a new aura – the aura of being holy scripture – that they were seen as proof texts for a resurrection of the body. We need not follow these arguments, but we might think that preserved in the Bible is a set of stories intended to demonstrate that Jesus had risen from the dead. What they may have meant by this will be examined later.

Then there are the appearances of Jesus to his disciples. It is almost impossible to take these accounts at the superficial level of factual reporting. The inconsistencies are not as clear as in the stories of the empty tomb, but are present at more subtle levels. To quote E. G. Selwyn again – as a conservative theologian he accepts the fundamentalist position that the resurrection was an historical event: "The most fruitful line of approach to this problem is not that of enforcing a harmony upon the different narratives, but rather that of emphasizing the distinct interests and standpoints of the several evangelists. Each evangelist's mind is dominated by his own special purpose and conception, and it is precisely at the close of his story that we shall expect that purpose to be most plain." Just so. Each writer has his own point of view, and it affects the way he tells the tale. The insight that Selwyn gives here is that in order to understand the story we have to bear in mind what the writer was trying to do. In trying, he tells his tale, his parable, his myth.

More revealing than any disharmony between the events of

one story and those of another is the way in which Jesus' risen body is described. Helen Milton again:

> Some of the stories about Jesus' resurrection appearances also seem to present a naïve picture which suggests that Jesus' flesh and blood body was resuscitated. In John's account, Thomas is said to have felt the wounds suffered by Jesus on the cross. In Luke the risen Jesus is supposed to have said, "A spirit does not have flesh and blood as you see I have." After this we read that he ate some broiled fish. I have always found it difficult to take these details literally, especially when they are combined with strange sudden appearances and disappearances of the risen Lord, even through closed doors. There's no agreement in these stories on where Jesus appeared, in Galilee, Jerusalem, or both, or to whom he appeared first, Peter or Mary Magdalen. But the Gospels and Paul do agree, implicitly, that these appearances were limited to the followers of Christ. And Paul equates his experience of seeing the risen Lord with those which others had in the days shortly after Jesus' death. This seems to indicate that he understood all of them as spiritual experiences. Neither he nor anyone else suggests in the New Testament that such an experience is a necessary part of Christian life.

II

If we are not committed to taking these narratives of the empty tomb and the appearances to the disciples as precise recordings of events, we are liberated to enter a deeper response. If the writer is trying to spell out the underlying meaning of the story, then we have to meet him at a more personal level than if he is simply reciting a series of incidents.

If anything is real to people today it is death, which is inescapable. The notion that the resurrection stories assure us that our souls are immortal, that our earthly bodies will one day rise from the dead, or that the promise is one of "pie in the sky when I die," is one that is acceptable to fewer and fewer people. One of the doctrines that many Christians can no longer believe in is that of the after-life. For myself, it is a doctrine that has no meaning. As I look back over my life, I can discover no occasion on which

I have ever taken it into account when making decisions. In all important events, when I have been considering the most important factors, I have thought of my family, the consequences for their future and mine, the income available, the comforts and discomforts involved, the possible achievements, the sort of people I would be meeting, the nature of the authority structure into which I would be moving, the element of freedom involved in the work, and so on. These were the important decisions calling for the most important reasons. At no time can I recall ever having thought to myself: "In making this decision, I must have in mind my after-life." My suspicion is that very few people do. Yet if it were truly believed, I can imagine no more important doctrine, no more important factor to take into account. In fact, the few people I know who really do seem to believe in an after-life put it in a position of priority. In making their decisions, they are acutely and ceaselessly aware that one day, beyond the grave, they will have to meet their maker and will then be judged.

The modern Christian sits lightly to the belief in an after-life. He may be willing to make a verbal assent, but he will do no more. In this, I believe that he is in the company of early writers like Paul. To them, resurrection was an eternal *now*, not something in the past or in the future. Life continues; death is always present, but life goes on. There is no end to the life-giving reality of nature. I look at people I know and realize that we can never die. Whatever life I have lived, the world is different because I have done so. Nothing can ever be the same again. There is no way of knowing what events would or would not have happened if I had not been born. I am eternal. But I am eternal here and now. C. S. Lewis asserted that the only point at which time and eternity meet is the present. It is in the present that we know both time and eternity; it is in the present that we are eternal. We do not die. Perhaps we cannot die. But if you ask me to believe that my body or my personality will somehow come alive again beyond the grave, you ask me to believe something that eludes me – something that I can no longer accept.

Because I once did accept it, mentally at any rate, I can understand that there are Christians who interpret the resurrection stories as historical, who are convinced that here is the pattern for their own life after death. This attitude must surely be accepted. In the pluralism of modern Christianity, there is no reason why one should try to win over another group to one's own convictions. If a person knows that he will live again, then in some way he will, though I cannot imagine how. I know that I will die, and that I will not be seen again in this world or any other. But I believe in resurrection, the eternal nature of living. This the traditional Christian must surely accept, even if he cannot imagine it.

III

The empty tomb and the resurrection appearances do not end the discussion. The great evidence for the historical nature of the events is the change that took place in the life of the apostles. In an early, pre-Robinson book, I wrote:

> On Good Friday, the apostles were weak and timid men who, thinking that Jesus Christ had failed, forsook him and fled. Less than a week later, these same men are meeting together once more, though in secret. After Pentecost, they suddenly develop into courageous leaders of the Church, willing to meet persecution and death for their faith. What made such a tremendous change? They themselves said it was the Resurrection; and this would seem to be the only possible explanation.

I wonder.

In 1956, Leon Festinger, Henry W. Riecken, Jr., and Stanley Schachter wrote a book *When Prophecy Fails* (Minneapolis: University of Minnesota Press, 1956), a report on a research project at the University of Minnesota. Their findings may suggest to some readers another way of interpreting the evidence. The writers were not concerned with the resurrection narratives; nor do I offer here more than a point of departure. I think that it is a good point of departure, certainly a necessary corrective to any over-confidence concerning the evidence; but I do not wish to be interpreted as implying any more. The differences between the type of research undertaken and the resurrection stories are many and, though I do not believe that they are necessarily significant, they might seem to be so.

"Suppose," suggest the authors, "an individual believes something with his whole heart; suppose further that he has a commitment to this belief and that he has taken irrevocable actions because of it; finally, suppose that he is presented with evidence, unequivocal and undeniable evidence, that his belief is wrong: what will happen? The individual will frequently emerge, not only unshaken, but even more convinced of the truth of his beliefs than ever before. Indeed, he may even show a new fervour for convincing and converting other people to his view."

The researchers tried to explain this increased fervour, and they suggested that there were five conditions under which it takes place:

1. The belief must be held with deep conviction and must be relevant to the life of the believer.

2. The person holding the belief must be so committed to it that he has undertaken some commitment that is difficult to undo.

3. The belief must be sufficiently specific and sufficiently concerned with the real world so that events may refute the belief.

4. The evidence must occur, and must be seen by the believer to have occurred.

5. The individual believer must have social support for continuing his belief in spite of the evidence.

These five conditions have frequently been satisfied in history, very often when some Christians have foretold the end of the world, or the millennium. A typical example was Montanus, who in the second century declared that the Second Coming of Our Lord was at hand. "Nor," wrote the historian Hughes, quoted in *When Prophecy Fails*, "did the delay of the second Advent put an end to the movement. On the contrary, it gave it new life and form." Another is the frequently altered forecasts put out by the sect now called Jehovah's Witnesses.

To explain why there is a vast increase in proselytizing after a prediction or a conviction has been disproven, the authors introduce the notion of dissonance. Dissonance arises when a person finds that two opinions, beliefs, or items of knowledge do not fit together. "For example, a cigarette smoker who believes that smoking is bad for his health has an opinion that is dissonant with the knowledge that he is continuing to smoke."

When dissonance occurs, we have to reduce it. Take the case of those who foretell that the end of the world will occur at a certain time. The end of the world does not so occur. What happens? The failure of the prophecy introduces a most painful dissonance; the new event (that the world has not ended) is in powerful dissonance with the belief in the prediction, with the rest of the creed into which the prediction has been built, and with the actions the believer has taken because of his belief. If the commitment has been great and the belief itself of major importance, then the believer, faced with this intolerable dissonance, must do something to eliminate or reduce it. The obvious way is to abandon the prediction or the previous belief, preserve such of it as is consistent with the new events, and "return to a more usual existence." Sometimes, however, the "behavioural commitment to the belief system is so strong that almost any other course of action is preferable. It may even be less painful to tolerate the dissonance than to discard the belief and admit one has been wrong."

Alternatively, the dissonance can be reduced or eliminated by pretending that nothing has gone wrong. Unfortunately, the event is sometimes too clear to be passed off in this way. Perhaps the date was wrong, and they begin to set another date. The most usual way, however, is to "find reasonable explanations, very often ingenious ones, for the failure of their prediction." Such rationalization, however, requires support from others in order to make the new explanation make sense. "Fortunately, the disappointed believer can usually turn to others in the same movement who have the same dissonance and the same pressure to reduce it. Support for the new explanation is, hence, forthcoming and the members of the movement can recover somewhat from the shock of disconfirmation."

If the belief has been big enough and the event clear enough, the dissonance may still be too great. "There is, however, a way in which the remaining dissonance can be reduced. *If more and more people can be persuaded that the system of belief is correct, then clearly it must, after all, be correct.* It is for this reason that we observe the increase in proselytizing following disconfirmation. If the proselytizing proves successful, then by gathering more adherents and effectively surrounding himself with supporters, the believer reduces dissonance to the point where he can live with it."

IV

The researchers, arriving at these conclusions from an examination of historical and contemporary events, were soon able to undertake first-hand research into the matter. "One day at the end of September the Lake City *Herald* carried a two-column story, on a back page, headlined: PROPHECY FROM PLANET. CLARION CALL TO CITY: FLEE THAT FLOOD. IT'LL SWAMP US ON DEC. 21, OUTER SPACE TELLS SUBURBANITE." It turned out that a Mrs. Keech had received many messages from outer space, sent to her by superior beings, who had been visiting the earth in flying saucers. The authors, reading the paper, decided to join Mrs. Keech's group and observe what happened at first hand. They remained with her until the whole episode came to an end.

About nine months before the newspaper story, Mrs. Keech had received her first messages, warning the people on earth of the coming cataclysm. She told her friends and soon had a small following of believers. Among them was a Dr. Armstrong, from a nearby college town, who organized a group of believing students who met at his home. Dr. Armstrong and his wife also visited Mrs. Keech regularly.

During the fall, the two groups met to prepare for the final destruction of the earth and to find ways of escape. "As December 21 drew near, some members gave up their jobs, others gave away their possessions, and nearly all made public declarations of their convictions." Except for one interview, Mrs. Keech had confined her proselytizing to friends and acquaintances, and Dr. Armstrong had severely limited the number in his group. During

October and November, there was an increasingly strict secrecy about their beliefs and activities. In fact, there was a great resistance to taking members, and great resistance to publicity. In answer to the barrage of telephone calls which came to Mrs. Keech's house as December 21 approached, the consistent reply was, "No comment."

By the late afternoon of December 20, the group began to make its last preparations. Mrs. Keech had received a message instructing them to be ready to receive a visitor, who would arrive at midnight and escort them to a parked flying saucer which would whisk them away from the flood to a place of safety, presumably in outer space. The group carefully prepared and rehearsed the rituals they would adopt when the visitor arrived, and the passwords they would give in order to enter the flying saucer. They then removed all metal from their persons.

> The last ten minutes before midnight were tense ones for the group assembled in Mrs. Keech's living room. They had nothing to do but sit and wait, their coats on their laps. In the silence two clocks ticked loudly, one about ten minutes faster than the other. When the fast clock pointed to 12:05, someone remarked about the time aloud. A chorus of people replied that midnight had not yet come. One member affirmed that the slower clock was correct; he had set it himself only that afternoon. It showed only four minutes before midnight.
>
> Those four minutes passed in complete silence except for a single utterance. When the [slower] clock on the mantel showed only one minute remaining before the guide to the saucer was due, Mrs. Keech exclaimed in a strained, high-pitched voice: "And not a plan has gone astray." The clock chimed twelve, each stroke painfully clear in the expectant hush. The believers sat motionless.
>
> One might have expected some visible reaction, as the minutes passed. Midnight had come and gone, and nothing had happened. The cataclysm itself was less than seven hours away. But there was little to see in the reactions of the people in that room. There was no talking, no sound of any sort. People sat stock still, their faces seemingly frozen and expressionless.
>
> Gradually, painfully, an atmosphere of despair and con-

fusion settled over the group. They re-examined the prediction and the accompanying messages. Dr. Armstrong and Mrs. Keech reiterated their faith. The believers mulled over their predicament and discarded explanation after explanation as unsatisfactory. At one point, toward 4:00 A.M., Mrs. Keech broke down and sobbed that there were some who were beginning to doubt, but that the group must beam light to those who needed it most, and that they must hold together. The rest of the believers were losing their composure, too. They were all visibly shaken and many were close to tears. It was now almost 4:30 A.M. and still no way of handling the disconfirmation had been found. By now, most of the group were talking openly about the failure of the escort to come at midnight. The group seemed near dissolution.

But this atmosphere did not continue long. At about 4:45 A.M., Mrs. Keech summoned everyone to attention, announcing that she had just received a message. She then read aloud these momentous words: "For this day it is established that there is but one God of Earth and He is in thy midst, and from his hand thou hast written these words. And mighty is the word of God – and by His word have ye been saved – for from the mouth of death have ye been delivered and at no time has there been such a force loosed upon the Earth. Not since the beginning of time upon this Earth has there been such a force of Good and Light as now floods this room and that which has been loosed within this room now floods the entire Earth. As thy God has spoken through the two who sit within these walls has he manifested that which he has given thee to do. . . ."

The atmosphere in the group changed abruptly and so did their behaviour. Within minutes after she had read the message explaining the disconfirmation, Mrs. Keech received another message instructing her to publicize the explanation. This they began to do, calling newspapers and radio stations. They talked freely to reporters and enthusiastically proselytized the visitors and the inquirers who called at the house.

The situation worked out differently for those members of the college group who had gone home instead of to Mrs. Keech's house. They had no people of like mind to turn to, and they either gave up their beliefs completely or found their convictions much weakened; they attempted no proselytizing.

It would be absurd to suggest that there is an exact parallel between this incident and the story of the behaviour of the Christians after the crucifixion; but there is enough of a parallel to admit of some questions. We may look at the five conditions set out by Festinger, Riecken, and Schachter in relation to the resurrection story.

1. There was a clear belief that Jesus was the Messiah. There was no thought of resurrection, and no suggestion was made other than that the disciples were surprised by the turn events took.

2. Their belief in the Messianic role of Jesus was relevant to their lives, and they had committed themselves to it, some of them even giving up their life's work. To turn back on these actions would prove difficult, as Peter discovered when he denied Jesus.

3. The belief was not specifically connected with any one predicted event – the big difference between the spiritual narrative and the five analytic points raised in *When Prophecy Fails*.

4. Although there was no specific indication as to how or when Jesus' Messianic role was to be established, one event could, in fact, end it: the death of their leader under insulting conditions. The fourth point may be taken then as implying the third.

5. The disciples sought and found communal support. Their first reaction was to give up. They fled, they huddled in failure. When the women visited the tomb, they did not go with anything other than sadness in their hearts to anoint a dead body.

Earlier in this chapter, I pointed out the difficulties of accepting the Biblical parables and stories as if they were factual narratives. But the general impression is clear enough. After the crucifixion, there was a great sense of failure, of complete loss.

How did the disciples react? The rationalization comes slowly. It does not necessarily happen at one meeting. But once it is detected, it is quickly seized. Jesus is not dead at all! He is risen! Quickly the enthusiasm mounts. But the sharing of a new conviction is not enough. There must be more. The dissonance is still too great. The apostles had done very little proselytizing before. There were no missionary journeys of the type Paul would undertake. Jesus was followed wherever he went. He won converts, but he did not seem anxious to do so. On many occasions he urged secrecy among those he helped. Certainly there is no evidence whatever that the disciples set up a body of believers other than the one that gathered naturally as Jesus moved around Palestine. But they find themselves in the middle of a completely new situation. The cross has intervened, a dramatic signal of failure. Now, after a short period of despair, a deep hope has come to them. They can show that the cross, far from being a disaster, is in reality a success, the final and ultimate triumph. Through it the world has been saved, and they proceed to save the world with it. "If more and more people can be persuaded that the system of belief is correct, then clearly it must after all be correct."

Naturally there are differences between a research account and the Biblical story or parable, but there are enough similarities to suggest a provisional inquiry as to how much of the resurrection story, followed so quickly by proselytizing, is an attempt by the followers of Jesus to reduce the dissonance created by his death on the cross. To do so undermines nothing of what has been said about the significance of the resurrection to them or to us. For the big difference between the research account and the resurrection story is the fact that Mrs. Keech's prediction was comparatively trivial; the significance of the empty tomb and the appearances is great. It would be fascinating if some research could be undertaken in which the prediction or belief was of major significance and not slightly comic; but we may guess, with some reason, that even if this were so the five points outlined in *When Prophecy Fails* would be met.

VI

The significance of the resurrection is great. In their rationalizations to prove that the cross instead of a defeat had really been a victory, the apostles were not rationalizing from an absurd belief into an absurd alternative. The death on the cross was real. Jesus died. His death was inevitable, given the circumstances of a rebel who opposed the leaders of church and state and stirred up the people into independence. It had always happened before; it will always happen again. He declared himself to be truly and fully man, and he got in the way of those who wished to use men and ride them to their own advantage. He was truly man, and he died. But his death was only one facet of human history. How much of the feeling for resurrection, the constant resurging of new life, stems from the apostles' rationalizing and how much from the event itself we shall never know; but it is of little importance. Rationalizing, though it may be observed as an attempt to escape dissonance, may produce a consonance which is true in itself and to life. Because I rationalize does not mean that I move into error. It simply means that the precise event that I looked for did not take place as I looked for it. So I have to explain it and, in the explanation, I may stumble upon new truths. It is surely not too much to suggest that men, who had been in touch with such a man as Jesus, would not be so completely bereft of their senses that they would miss the signals of death and rebirth. The cross was the end and may still be seen as the end. It was also the centre and may still be seen as the centre. To the Christian, Jesus is still alive in the world, seen or unseen, known or unknown, followed or ignored.

Perhaps the greatest significance of the apostles' actions, so interpreted, may be, as James Fisk points out, the breath-taking way in which human beings are able to come together in unity and, even out of disaster, develop a common life. Here is complete failure and death; and yet, within weeks, they are all alive again. They have found a new foundation upon which to build their lives. If, indeed, the apostles, faced with a clear disconfirmation of the event they had expected, turned instead to a proclamation of resurrection, then we have a greater support for the continual rising of the human spirit than the old interpretations.

VII

An afterword. It is obvious that the events of the scriptures can, with some modifications, be interpreted as history; and that a majority of Christians will continue to believe that Jesus really rose in his body from the dead, though they may legitimately evade saying in what way. The questions raised in this chapter may, though I have not pressed them hard, still sound completely absurd to some readers. If so, then that is the way it is. Yet there are many loyal members of our Churches who, though filled with happy songfulness at Easter time, have never really believed the empty tomb, have taken most of the resurrection stories with a pinch of salt, and have found great difficulty in understanding exactly how Jesus did rise and whether the story, as read out and preached about in Church, really makes sense.

So far as hopes of an after-life are concerned, they vary according to the nature of the person. One side of everyone would like to live forever. If we can judge from men's actions, a belief in an after-life does not interfere very much with everyday behaviour. Few neighbours in the Toronto suburb in which I live conduct themselves as if they were convinced that they might meet their Maker tonight. And if there is any distinction here between churchgoer and absentee, it does not meet the eye.

CHAPTER VI

A New Book Called the Bible

I

One of the biggest temptations that beset men in their search for life is the hope that, somewhere, somehow, a halt may be called. The prospect of a search that never ends, the discovery of questions which will never be finally answered, though exciting at times, can create despair, especially in minds that are not happy unless they arrive at a destination.

The result is that, throughout history, man has selected certain points and said: "So far, no further." The longing for a final and complete Truth, a final and complete Goodness, a final and complete Beauty, a final and complete Purity, makes us suppose that these absolutes are achievable. There is, however, no sign at all that they are achieved in the present; the future offers little hope of it; and so we are left with the past. Long ago, we conclude, there was once a Golden Age, when perfection was known.

Man invents a God who is perfect, changeless. As we have seen, such a God inevitably becomes remote and detached, but he satisfies the need for complete and utter perfection somewhere in the universe. Man's longings are still not completely satisfied. He would feel better if he thought that such perfection was possible on the earth. Once more, the present looks bleak because it is peopled with real, imperfect people; the future is uncertain; but the past is possible. There was a time when man was once perfect. In those days, he walked in a Garden of Eden, a flawless being until he sinned. This is a beautiful dream which, because everything we know of man belies it, is set in a prehistoric era. If it happened before the dawn of history, nobody can produce data to contradict us and, if they do not accept our story, we can accuse them of disbelief, irreligion, or any other thoughtless indictment which our age happens to allow.

There is something still unreal about this, however, and so we invent a Perfect Man. He does not err and he cannot sin. This produces problems, for the man has of necessity to be described. If he lives in history and is reported extensively, he makes mistakes. This is speedily dealt with by saying that he was limited by the knowledge of his day, but he did not err spiritually. This satisfies the hunger for a perfection that is not intellectual but moral. Furthermore, there is no way of disputing it. By definition, the Perfect Man is perfect. Therefore, if you feel that he was less than fully good, you must be mistaken. Everything he said and did is tested against the rule of perfection. He cannot have erred morally; therefore, when faced with an incident which suggests that he did not err normally, we have to explain it away.

Thus in response to the story of the Phoenician woman, used in Chapter IV, it is said that Jesus cannot have been prejudiced, nor can he have been unkind to the woman. Therefore he was not unkind; therefore he knew all the time that he wanted to help her and heal her daughter. He calls her a dog. This sounds cruel, and Jesus could clearly not be cruel. Therefore he was not cruel and there must be some innocent explanation for his words. Perhaps he was referring to attractive little "puppy dogs" or said it with a twinkle in his eye. Even this, of course, explains nothing. For if he really knew what she needed and was prepared to grant it, this was no time to be bandying theological niceties about who were the chosen people; and twinkle or no twinkle, it seems an inappropriate time to make light jokes. If anything, the respectable explanations insult his character more than the simple acknowledgment that he was, in fact, prejudiced. This, at least, enables him to learn and show that he is willing to deal with a mistake. But this is always the trap into which the perfectionist falls. Nothing must be at fault, and so explanations of incidents are made that do not explain and, sooner or later, are seen by the normal listener to be the evasions they really are.

To the Perfect God and the Perfect Man are added other

beings and institutions which cannot err. Mother Church claims the privilege for herself; it is claimed for the popes. Difficulties mount as palpable mistakes are made in the moral sphere. They are held in check by arguments other than direct confrontations between objector and answerer. Until recently, it was considered disloyal, almost heretical, for a Roman Catholic to question the infallibility of the pope.

As there are no perfections in the world, never have been, and perhaps never will be, if we intend to believe in a Perfect Being or institution, we must take care that no facts are available for examination. It is advisable to put the perfection out in space beyond the reach of man's instruments, or back in time before history. As soon as the perfection comes within the range of our instruments or within history, then we can only maintain it when we are able to apply such heavy sanctions that those who do not believe it will be afraid to say so.

II

Another of the major ingredients of human existence is the desire for magic. Almost everything we achieve is at the expense of effort, and we long for the short cut. Acts of magic are quickly attributed to the divine perfection. We are short of food. There is no time to grow it. The magic wand is waved; manna appears. Even within the last century, the Mormons spoke about such miracles. Their crops were being devoured by a plague of caterpillars. The faithful prayed. Next morning, they saw a huge flock of seagulls devouring the caterpillars – a flock of seagulls in the heart of America! They were saved by the magic of God.

The same desire for magic intrudes into the narratives of Jesus' life. Most of the healing he performs comes as a natural example of a fully integrated man giving confidence to people with illnesses which are notoriously psychosomatic – paralysis, epilepsy, and so forth. There is no magic here. Nor is there magic when some of the other events take place. But, as described by the narrators in the New Testament, the magical element is stressed. Water is turned into wine for the satisfaction of a wedding party, the new wine tasting better than the original. The magician is at work. St. John calls it a "sign." Five loaves and two small fishes feed a crowd of four or five thousand, to say nothing of women and children. When they have all eaten, the scraps fill twelve large baskets. The body of Lazarus is found so far gone that there is fear of a stench. Jesus brings him back to life. Magic. The short cut.

Part of magic is the reciting of certain forms of words in a certain way. The words themselves need not have meaning, but the incarnation must be accurate. Jesus himself played the game of magic when, before he cured the blind man, he spat on the ground and made a paste with his spittle, spread it on the man's eyes, and told him to wash in the pool of Siloam. All of the events have natural explanations which have been given in modern times; and certainly they may be duplicated in other ages, including our own. The only point suggested here is that the writers present these events in magical terms.

III

Both of these strong human desires – for perfection and for magic – are closely related; and they find a home in the Bible. The Bible is often treated as a magical book used for purposes of incantation. During the past four years, my work has involved me in writing curriculum materials for the Anglican Church of Canada. Before being revised and printed, these materials were tested for several years in over forty parishes. The teachers were asked to give as detailed reactions as they could to the material that was supplied to them. They did so with such thoroughness that the writers could have nothing but praise for the way the work was done.

In response to the first year's materials, one of the chief complaints made by teachers was that there was "not enough Bible." This was an interesting point because our own reactions were that we had provided roughly the same amount of Biblical material as our old courses had, which were generally acknowledged to be satisfactory from this point of view. We took a look at the old materials and discovered a possible reason. Each lesson had begun with a text. Most of the children's materials included a picture of a Biblical character painted in a sentimental Victorian style. In the course of the lesson, the Bible story was referred to. Finally, certain texts were recommended for daily Bible reading or memorizing, though we could find no evidence of their being widely used. It was not, therefore, a question of the Bible being utilized so much as the right incantation being said. In our new materials, the Bible was offered as one resource among many. The teacher, though she would probably use it, was not obligated to do so. She could, if she preferred, choose a more modern illustration. Furthermore, the children were encouraged to ask questions, and we provided none of the old magical answers. Had Jesus been unfair to Martha? Had the elder brother of the Prodigal been treated unreasonably? We suggested that the children should answer these questions for themselves. We suggested that there were no right answers, no interpretations which could be said to be the Church's reply. Some of the teachers responded warmly to this freedom of interpretation; others dried up and withered away, feeling that a Bible that did not supply its answers clearly was no Bible.

The desire for a book of incantations also took a more subtle form. Some of the manuals had repeated certain themes to see if different methods of operation would receive different reception. In one of the grades, there were two topics, fairly widely separated, which dealt with precisely the same subject. One of these topics was rated very high by the teachers, the other very low. Yet they both had the same theme. Why the difference? The reasons given by the teachers included: not enough Bible in the second topic. A check showed that, in fact, the popular topic had less Biblical guidance than the unpopular one. At first sight, we might have deduced that the people did not like the Bible. But this did not make sense. A closer examination showed that the unpopular topic suffered from two defects: the gimmicks recommended were not easily workable, and the explanatory columns were obscure. In the popular topic, the gimmicks were easy to work and well received by children; the explanations were clearly written. We now had a possible solution. The teachers found the second topic had fallen flat. The children were bored; the teachers were bored. Something had gone wrong. The reason was that the writers had muffed their work. But this did not occur to the teachers. Perhaps they remembered a clergyman complaining about lack of Bible teaching; perhaps they had read a blast in their diocesan paper. At all events, they grasped the magical explanation: there was no Bible, so the topic had failed.

In a book as short as this, the illustration has been abbreviated and over-simplified. The conclusion, however, was placed beyond dispute by the close research that followed the initial discoveries. The Bible is regarded as magic by many Christians. When an evangelist says he believes in the Bible, he means that he accepts every word of it. There is no room for critical analysis, doubt, or questioning. Radio's hot-line consultants frequently face the querulous arguments of listeners whose claim is that they believe in the Bible. If we believe in the Bible, they say, we *must* believe in capital punishment, hell, and religious education in schools. The incantation is delivered; the magic is achieved.

Its achievement depends upon the belief that the Bible is perfect. It is the Word of God which may not be questioned. Some traditionalists, perhaps most, are prepared to question the texts, reinterpret the myths, analyze the authorship and dates of different books, query the accuracy of certain passages, agree that certain verses are intrusions from later writers. Few, faced with what they feel to be the original text, are prepared to say that they disagree with the Bible, disagree with a certain prophet, disagree with Jesus, or disagree with Paul. In some of these cases, as that of Jesus, there is a double perfection at stake. For Paul and the prophets, it is the fact that a statement is in the Bible that gives it its cachet.

Such a belief runs headlong into the convictions held by the modern Christian pluralist, and he finds increasing tensions within himself. Though there is every reason why he should be willing to hold side-by-side the belief that the Bible may err, and that it is also infallible, in practice he is confused. Trying to find close relationships with all men, of whatever religion, faith, or philosophy, and trying to feel that all attitudes are justified, he is nagged by the thought that the Bible is perfect. Even when he has detached himself from the Church, he can still be clobbered into submission by a Bible-quoter. In every argument he enters with a Fundamentalist,* he finds that the other man has one more text to throw at his head. He is impressed. Can the other man have something, after all? The Bible is surely true. Finding that he constantly falls short in his arguments, sometimes taking refuge in anger, he wonders what is wrong with him.

There is, of course, nothing wrong. He has simply been faced with the old Monism† in a particularly entrenched form. Man, says the traditional Christian, needs a core to which his various actions may be related. Such a core, both inside and outside the Christian community, but especially in the Protestant churches, is the Bible. Here is the book that unifies all Christians, that provides man with the answers he needs. In it, preacher upon preacher finds the answers to the miseries of this present age. Nor is this to be despised. The Bible writers were great men, with great insights, who saw through sham and hypocrisy, who understood the hearts of men and the depths of their being. The Bible is naturally filled with a wisdom that sets up a sympathetic echo in anyone's heart, whether he be a Christian or an old-fashioned atheist. The only contention here is that these writers were not infallible; that they could make mistakes; that they did make mistakes.

In our new "hominized" world, the world described in Chapter II, we do not need a single core. We live in a pluralized society which is committed neither to the social forms laid out with declared divine sanction in the Bible nor to the world view set out as under the control of the God of history nor, in fact, to any spiritually controlled unity.

In Chapter II, I mentioned Harvey Cox's quotation from Johann Metz. The Bible itself bears witness to Metz's "pluralism of consciousness." Within its pages, taken as a whole or within the words of a single writer, we are presented with men who lived

---

*The Oxford Dictionary defines "Fundamentalism" as: "Strict adherence to traditional [Protestant] tenets (e.g., the literal inerrancy of Scripture) held to be fundamental to Christianity; adherence to traditional views of any kind." In this chapter, I am specifically concerned with the Fundamentalist who believes that every word of the Bible is literally true.

†Webster defines "Monism" as: "The doctrine that there is only one ultimate substance or principle, whether mind, matter, or some third thing that is the basis of both. As distinct from Dualism and Pluralism."

out the most varied tendencies and impulses. What view, for example, does the Bible take of life after death? There is none. From the cynical despair of Ecclesiastes, through the moderate hope of Job and the confident generalized commitments of Paul to the specifics of Revelation, there is nothing that provides a unified focus; and, on closer examination, the individual authors present only the appearance of a single point of view.

When we step outside the Bible and look at it through the eyes of a modern reader, the conglomeration of tendencies and impulses multiplies at a fantastic rate. A modern man, set among others who share very little of his character and motivations, and realizing that he himself is neither unified nor whole, responds to a grouping of scriptural characters who have little in common and who are torn apart within themselves.

Until the present age, Christians felt under an obligation to discover a unity in their lives. They found it in the concept of God. The Bible was thought to capture and encapsulate this philosophical concept. Here was the Word of God, the words of God. Clearly, then, there was a unity that girded together all its parts and gave to man a revelation which was to be set at the core of his faith, though not the exclusive core it nearly became after the Reformation.

Initially, the Church offered the Bible as such a core to life while at the same time it permitted free reading and interpretation of it. The results, by the standards of the time, were disastrous. Different conclusions were reached, different types of analysis used, different responses and applications made, and even different books and texts produced. To the older theologians, as to many today, such pluralism was synonymous with chaos, and that chaos had to be reshaped into order, organization, and proper decency.

This might have been done by examining the texts and separating the acceptable from the unacceptable. It was, in fact, tried, and it may have been for this reason that such books as *The Shepherd of Hermas* were rejected, because the bishops felt that it would muddle simple people, and that other books would do a similar job better. Yet this method could only be used after a limited fashion, as Marcion had found out to his cost; when he

97

suggested that the only Bible needed for Christians was the New Testament, he was condemned as a heretic.

An alternative approach was to accept the texts as they came, with all their embarrassing pluralism, and to make sure that only a few people – committed in their allegiance to a supreme human authority who claimed divine saction – had the interpreting of them, and ultimately their mere reading. Even this turned out to be more difficult than had been anticipated, and it was left to the Middle Ages to bring to perfection the happy expedient of ensuring the unity of the Bible by hiding it from the people in a foreign language which only the most reliable Catholics could understand. The solution still obtains unsuccessfully in Protestant circles that retain the King James Version.

IV

In our modern society, this can no longer take place. There is still censorship, both official and unofficial, which is not easy to identify but which ensures that the Bible is treated as if it were an idol or a talisman. Thus certain Baptists in Canada solemnly burned the curriculum which they had bought from the United Church because, they said, it did not believe in the Bible. In point of fact, the curriculum had merely raised some mild questions concerning the mythology of such books as Genesis.

The censorship, however, operates in areas that are constantly decreasing and among people who become fewer in number. Modern man has access to the Bible in any way that suits him. He can read interpretations by a whole range of writers, from the deepest fundamentalist to the freest cynic; and what he reads paints a picture that not only tells how foolish it is to expect any certainty, but proclaims the constantly shifting patterns of truthful experience. The pluralism of the original Bible writers has now been multiplied many times – by scribes, editors, translators, and interpreters, to name but a few – until at last it is multiplied by the pluralism of the modern reader set in the pluralism of his society. If there is any unity in this, it is clearly beyond the range of any man or group of men to decide or define.

To pretend to such a core or unifying principle implies that one has limited the number of facts at which one is willing to look and made a unity out of *them*. For those who are willing to make this drastic reduction of reality, there may still be a unified core to existence. For the rest, it is impossible.

One of the big discoveries that we may now make is that we are quite incapable of having all things at our disposal. We have already discovered this in the world of science, where we are learning new responsibilities and new controls, but also realizing their limitations. We can now see that the Bible is similarly placed. Because it is our book, to be used in any way which suits us, we can find new areas unknown before, and offer new questions and new analyses which were formerly denied as being heretical, indecent, or even blasphemous. All this opens our eyes to new aspects of the Bible previously closed to us. At the same time, it proclaims our limitations. Under the old theories, it was possible to manipulate the Bible and to do so successfully. To debate with a deep fundamentalist is not to be faced with a fool, but with a person who will win his arguments because his attitude to the Bible makes it possible for him to take the book and subdue it. So long as it is the single Word of God, infallibly proclaimed by a single voice to a single believer, then all is in the believer's grasp. But if the Bible is a multiplicity of voices, not all of them consistent; if it proclaims uncertainty and a constant shifting of patterns; if we are permitted to approach it without apology and with confident assurance of the pluralism within the book itself, within ourselves as individuals, and within society at large; then it is, indeed, a book that we cannot bring under our control.

V

A most interesting modern event is the shot in the arm the scriptures are receiving not so much from orthodox and conservative believers as from reformers, changers, and secularizers. This is reasonable because, as Harvey Cox establishes in *The Secular City*, the Bible itself gives clear signals towards reform, its messages being based on the need for change, freedom, and uncertainty.

The modern secular way of life is a product of Biblical pluralism. The modern Christian has, therefore, much to gain from reading the Bible. But he need feel under no compulsion to do so. To allow ourselves to be ashamed because we do not read the Bible more, or meditate more upon it, or know more about it, is to allow ourselves to be pushed backwards. If there is a unity of the Bible, it is as hidden from us as the unity of God, and there is no way in which we can pretend otherwise. It is simply one of the many contexts in which we live our lives. For many people, including Christians, it is no longer a context at all.

One of Marshall McLuhan's several million ideas offered in the realm of communications is the distinction between a "hot" medium and a "cool" medium. A "hot" medium, which McLuhan considers inferior, is that in which one side does all or most of the talking. This is the method by which a teacher lectures and hopes that the students are listening. Research has shown that, if this method is adopted, they learn nothing, or next to nothing. By contrast, a "cool" medium is one in which the learner is involved in setting the pattern of learning, so that the topic becomes a joint effort between teacher and learner. If this method is used, then the learning experience is livelier and more successful.

Apply this to the Bible. The Bible is concerned with life. If a teacher talks about life and declares the Bible's teaching about it, the student receives very little. He may learn it off by heart and be able to recite back texts, but he misses its real significance; and his fellow men, whom he tries to convert, are irritated by what they feel is a lack of perception. They are right. The fundamentalist has manipulated the Bible into a memorizable set of texts, which can only reflect a sadly small segment of the Bible's message, and that small segment over-simplified and regulated. The learner believes that he has learned his Bible; he has, in fact, played no part in the process and often becomes simply a censorious busybody. "Are you a religious bigot?" asks the modern Jewish pluralist on the radio, when challenged on the hot-line by a phone caller. It is the first question that rises to the mind when faced with a Christian who has simply learned his Bible off by heart.

If the life that is in the Bible is to be learned, it must be shared, and it is impossible to share it until one has freely entered into an examination of one's own life. Study of the Bible presupposes such a study and, if a group of people wish to understand what the Bible has to offer, they may need to spend many months talking about themselves. They may, as events turn out, never actually open the Bible; and perhaps this will be good. If they do open it, however, they will be part of it, and it will mean something.

Above all, the Bible must be offered to the modern Christian without any strings attached. He may take it or leave it as he thinks fit. There are many contexts in our lives, including religious ones, which are not necessarily made more vivid because the Bible is brought in. Where the Bible finds a natural home – as in the freedom marches in the United States – then it is a self-authenticating piece of work. Where it is used simply because we feel obligated to do so, then it becomes a drag. The nearly across-the-board boredom of so many Sunday School children is ample evidence of this.

VI

The discoveries we made in writing our new curriculum for the Anglican Church included the realization that the Bible was far from complete. If the Bible is to be a "cool" medium, if it is to be seen as relevant to the learner, then we must start with the sort of situation in which the learner normally finds himself. In topic after topic, having identified with students the problems they faced, we discovered that there was no Bible passage that would meet the situation.

We considered passages enunciating some general principle which, if enough intermediate steps were taken, could be shown to apply to the problem under discussion. This proved a failure. If the Bible is to mean something, there must be an immediacy about it. If we are going to answer a teenager's question about how to deal with an unintelligent father, it is no use quoting, "Honour thy father and thy mother," or referring to St. Paul. In any immediate sense, Paul is useless, for he tells the young teenager to obey his father; and this is the one piece of advice that makes no sense.

There are many modern situations for which there is no

parallel in the Bible at all. For example, when the Bible was being written the world was underpopulated. The only practical advice was "be fruitful and multiply." Every social custom was adapted to this end, and every encouragement was given to ensure that the race would carry on. Today we live in a world which is threatened with overpopulation. The advice we need now is to cease being fruitful and to multiply less. The Bible has nothing at all to say to us about this, because the problem never occurred to the writers, and they did not foresee the future.

More difficult to deal with are those passages in which the Bible gives advice which, right in its own day, is wrong now. The Bible, for example, was written when the pattern of the average family was an authoritarian one. The modern-style family was unknown. The advice given in the Bible sounds ridiculous to many families today. Though there remain those who feel that women should obey their husbands in all things, because the man is the head of the woman as God is his, they no longer represent the new family. The working housewife, the day nursery, the five-day school week, female emancipation, all these were unknown to the Bible writers. The advice they gave is therefore rarely appropriate. It is always authoritarian, and it cannot do other than harm when it is inflicted on a family that is not authoritarian.

VII

In spite of this, Christians even today become alarmed when it is suggested that the Bible need not be right. They suppose that the pattern of life there set out must be the best one for all ages, and that our modern habits, clearly in conflict with some of them, are wrong. There is sometimes a tendency to feel that an emancipated woman should be ashamed of herself because the Bible tells her to be submissive; or that modern children should be ashamed of themselves because they do not obey their parents.

A similar difficulty arises when we think of society in general. The whole nature of a trade union is that, at certain times, the servant should not only disobey his master, but make sure that the master obeys the servant. This disobedience is part of our national system; and, without it, society would be the poorer. On this subject, the Bible's advice is on the side of the employer. Not always so, of course, for Moses is encouraged to disobey his Egyptian masters; but, if you were looking for some Bible passage that would commend itself immediately to a trade unionist about to strike, you would have to look far.

The simple truth is that the Bible is not complete. It is not the last word on anything. It needs additions and corrections in the light of new events. Our present church services imply that God's Word finished at a certain point in history, so far as sacred scriptures are concerned. This is absurd. There is no reason why we should not turn to modern prophets as much as we do to the old. There are contexts in which *Lord of the Flies* is a more useful, perhaps a deeper, myth than that of Genesis; in which *Death of a Salesman* shows more insight than Jonah; in which Martin Luther King presents a more dramatic plea for the triumph of grace over law than the neurotic Paul.

VIII

Above all, we need to discover that the Bible is, among all its other strange intertwines of life and death, a book of many dreams. It is neither a classical portrait nor a chocolate-box ensemble but a surrealist work of art. Perhaps it is here that we have the most to learn, for modern man has not grasped the significance of his new art forms. He still reacts unsympathetically to painting, music, and dance which do not set out their convictions in a pictorial fashion. He still demands something he can recognize: a photographic painting (though the best photography has itself become surrealist); a clear tune to his music; an obvious meaning to his dance; a straight-forward story to his writing. He prefers fact to fiction, documentary to drama, and soap opera to tragedy. In the world of the Bible, it is going to prove a severe task to show that the material *is* surrealist. Fundamentalists and literalists are not limited to the sects. To teach the modern Canadian or American, with his puritan background, that dreams are more valuable than work is indeed a challenge, though the English experience makes it seem more reasonable. All this is fair enough; because those who do not perceive the dreams are perceiving other meanings in life, and the Bible is far too varied to represent any one mode of artistic expression. Fortunately, more and more *are* noting the dreams, and so the challenge towards change becomes less frightening. Above anything else, a dream is uncertain and fuzzy; when challenged for data, the dreamer has to paint metaphor by way of reply. This links up with the magnificent fuzziness of life as lived by so many, and the one reinforces the other. As people are encouraged to dream, they become real.

The dreams of the Bible dig deep. The stories of Genesis, taken as literal statements of fact, are interesting enough. As dreams, they shake the foundations of our being. All the sexual fantasies, the strong drives, the hatreds, hostilities, loves and passions, the taking and giving between fleshly men and women, all are present. When God threw Adam and Eve out of the Garden of Eden for no obvious reason – how wise the dreamer who portrayed obedience in terms of nonsense! – he placed an angel at the borderline so that man would never return. Nor should he want to. The Garden of Eden was a bore, as much a seduction to us as it was to Adam and Eve. And so we can move, through the dreams of the Prophets, the fantasies of the Song of Solomon (pornographic, as it is, by the laws of Ontario), to the dreams of Daniel and Revelation. Taken literally, at the level of proclaimed fact, how useless the last book is! Taken as a dream, the projected passions of a man who pulsed with energy, how new and vivid! We fill our dreams with ourselves. What a mixed-up, wonderful, extravagant man the writer showed himself to be! Perhaps, if we read him easily, as in a dream, letting it take us where it will, knowing that the details are symbols of his deepest hopes and dreads, we can find ourselves and learn to dream with him.

IX

The dreams of the Bible take many forms. The most obvious – and yet the most difficult to identify in our fundamentalist approach – is that of the parable or myth, the fictional story told for a purpose. Many Christians still suppose that a literal description of an event from the outside is somehow more accurate than an imaginative parable about human life.

The most popular example, and the best, is that of the Adam and Eve story. When a fundamentalist asks you: "Do you believe in the story of Adam and Eve?" he is not asking about your beliefs; he is asking whether Adam and Eve were historical figures, whether certain events took place which are described with precision in the book of Genesis, and whether there was a literal Garden from which, because of those events, a man and a woman were cast out. To the modern Christian, including some of the most conservative, this makes no sense. They do not think that the human race began in this way, nor do they think that the story of Adam and Eve is an historical document.

This is the first step in discovery. Unfortunately it often becomes the last. The person who refuses to accept the historicity of the Adam and Eve story often goes on to agree with the fundamentalist. He seems willing to say: "I do not believe the Bible when it says the human race began with Adam and Eve in the Garden of Eden." Yet is this what the Bible was saying? Even the early Church recognized that the story was a myth, a parable – the clothing of truths and insights in the language of a story. The writers of the book of Genesis are not interested in the scientific dawn of mankind; they are pressing upon us certain feelings that all men share. To tell a story is the best way to convey deep truths about ourselves. The old fairy tales, the old folk tales, the old saga poems did this. The writers of the Old and New Testaments did it. Jesus did it constantly. Once it is realized that the Bible is filled with such parables, that a myth is the best way to convey truth, then far from "disbelieving" the Bible we actually dig down to a deeper level. We may still not agree with the writer, but, if we understand the particular message he is conveying, we have come to a closer relationship with him, and this is what matters most. To take the stories of Genesis to be parables is to interpret the Bible at a more significant level than simply to take them as statements of historical "events." For if they are the latter, what have we? Simply a set of statements. The writer may have nothing in his mind except straight reportage; and the "events" may, or may not, matter. But if he had a deep concern for human beings and scratched the nerves of those concerns, then he is talking to us not across the ages but right now. The concerns of the Genesis story are the same as today: the sexuality of all human beings; man's drive for self-identification; his struggle after knowledge; his hatred, hostility, spite, and envy; the hopes that lift him to the rainbowed sky; and, above all, his need to stand erect and say, "I am a man." The dream is more real than the simple outline of dates and occasions; the parable is truer to life than the pedestrian recital of events.

A dream, however, is not "accurate" in the way the superficial description of an event is; nor is it infallible; nor is it to be believed, nor magical, nor perfect, nor the Word of God. It is a dream, no more. And taken with the other dreams of previous generations and those that come later — not the least our own — what more may we ask?

X

There may be nothing new in all this. The casual stance towards the Bible, the take-it-or-leave-it approach, may turn out to be simply a modern application of the attitude of the Eastern Orthodox Church. For them, the heart of life is (or was) the Liturgy, where everything is expressed and in which the Bible is merely one ingredient. For this reason, the modern Orthodox adherent sometimes surprises his Western neighbour by offering little or no lip-service to Bible reading at home. Why select one of life's many aspects over another? Yet it remains an important part, and can only be totally ignored to the loss of the whole.

This seems to be a Christian aim: that the Bible be seen as one of the resources we can use in order to discover who we are, and that we use it as seems best under the particular circumstances in which we find ourselves. If this is done, the Bible may occupy the forefront of our thinking; it may not be used at all. For most of us, I suspect, it will fall midway between the two extremes.

CHAPTER VII

The New Morality

I

One of the most illuminating radio programs on the North American continent is the "hot-line," in which listeners telephone to share their questions, complaints, and woes with a moderator. My own favourite is *Speak Your Mind*, conducted by Larry Solway on CHUM in Toronto.

Though it takes a wide variety of forms, there is one perennial subject: the New Morality. In practice, this usually means sex. As sex is at the heart of human life and, as sexual standards are easily applicable to the rest of our moral behaviour, this chapter will, for the most part, restrict itself to this one important area.

A careful listener to a "hot-line" quickly discovers that there are two philosophies concerning morality which far outnumber the rest. The first is the legalistic philosophy. To people who hold this view, there are rules that can be applied to every situation in life. The rules are clear-cut and may only be disobeyed under the most rigorous conditions. For these listeners, pre-marital and extra-marital sexual intercourse are always wrong; birth control is wrong; abortion is wrong; homosexuality is wrong. The reaction of the moderator to such callers varies. If the listener is, say, against birth control for religious reasons, usually Roman Catholic, he is kind. If, on the other hand, the listener appears to be expressing some antipathy towards the whole subject of sex, perhaps finding it distasteful or even "filthy," then the moderator rewards him with scathing and angry scorn. "You're just a narrow-minded prude," is a mild example. If the listener is judging, as many legalists are, he receives short shrift.

The second philosophical group, about the same size as the first, takes the view that every situation must be judged on its merits. Is pre-marital sexual intercourse wrong? They don't know. It depends upon the couple and the situation in which they are placed. Is it always right then? No: again it depends upon the couple. These listeners are warmly welcomed by the moderator, as indeed they deserve to be. They judge the subject under discussion not from any rule book but from whether good or harm is done to the people involved. They see the dangers and risks of pre-marital intercourse but think that it is often justified. They feel that more people should practise birth control than do so, but they would not like to make any sweeping generalizations. Sometimes they phone because some local court of law has taken a rigid line about an abortion, and an innocent person has been hurt. A girl, perhaps, has been raped, and the hospital authorities refuse to conduct an abortion because the law forbids it. Or an abortion is conducted by a doctor who feels that it is essential to the well-being of the girl involved. His decision offends the majesty of the law; he is charged, found guilty, and sentenced. Sometimes – though this is fortunately dying out – the sentence is accompanied by a gratuitous piece of moralizing from the bench. Either the sentence or the moralizing can trigger listeners into anger; they pick up their phones, and engage their anger with the moderator's long experience of the subject.

The moderator is patient with those who sympathize with the girl. Yet he also presents the other side of the case. Sometimes the listener appears to be condoning too much. He seems to be saying that anyone who wants an abortion should have one; the moderator points out the social consequences, the dangers to the general public, the second-guessing on the part of the girl, and so on. Nevertheless, whether or not he argues the specific point at issue, he supports the basic philosophy of the telephone caller: situation ethics. You have to judge each case on its merits. You may, or may not, find some "law" applicable. You know about the general law, often a good one; but you do not allow it to get in the way of helping the people involved. The moderator would support Joseph Fletcher's cab driver who said: "There are times when a man has to push his principles aside and do the right thing."

There is a third group, represented by only a few callers. This is the group which feels that there are no principles at all, that you should be able to do as you please. Sometimes such callers seem to be supporting the naïve philosophy of Hugh Heffner's *Playboy*, which regards women as disposable commodities. They are speedily demolished by the moderator. Sometimes they seem to feel that there is no possible way of discovering standards, and they are gently helped to perceive that they themselves, in fact, have some. Sometimes they feel that a clear conscience is a sufficient justification for an action. Yet they constitute a very small minority. On the few occasions when they call, the moderator takes a straight-forward line. There are, he points out, surely some principles by which we can work and live. We cannot do exactly what we want to do when we want to do it.

Although very few people take this last position, it is well-represented in the discussions, for it is deeply embedded in the minds of the legalists that this is what the second group really believes. To the legalist, there seems to be no difference between letting principles and laws act as servants and having no laws and principles at all. The legalist sees those who believe in the New Morality as having no morals, holding an "anything goes" philosophy and accepting no standards.

This confusion between the New Morality (which believes in situation ethics) and Antinomianism (which believes in no principles at all) is held to be partly the responsibility of Pope Pius XII. Joseph Fletcher, the author of *Situation Ethics* (Philadelphia: Westminster Press, 1966), the best book I know on the subject of the New Morality, writes:

> There has indeed been a "misplaced debate" about situation ethics, because so many have too quickly taken it to be *antinomian*. Their error, due to the oversimple judgment of some European theologians, first appeared officially in an allocution of Pius XII on April 18, 1952, in which the terms "existential" and "situational" were made synonymous. It was pointed out as a warning that such an ethic

could be used to justify birth control. Four years later "Situation Ethics" was labelled "The New Morality" and banned from all academies and seminaries.

Whatever the cause, there is no denying the result. In study groups, when the subject of the New Morality is discussed, it soon becomes apparent that the conservative element treat the subject as if it were the New *Im*morality. It soon becomes necessary to insist that any comparisons between old and new – and they are bound to be made – must be each to each. There was an Old Morality and there is a New Morality; there was an Old Immorality and there is a New Immorality. There is no point in trying to compare teenage violence in Central Park today with teenage prayer meetings at the City Temple in Victoria's day; there is no point, by way of riposte, in comparing our Victorian grandfathers sneaking off to the many starved prostitutes of Central London with the honest discussion of extra-marital sexual habits today. Any philosophy or way of life is practised and not practised at the same time. Anyone who thinks that the old standards of sexual morality were observed much further than the words used knows as little about the old days as the modern despiser who thinks that all Victorian men had unofficial harems. Anyone who thinks that the New Morality produces men and women of sublime honesty in their frank dealings with each other is as dreamy as the person who thinks that modern young people only leave their bed in order to move to the next one.

Joseph Fletcher astutely pinpoints the absurdity of trying to score points in this fashion when he quotes Lindsey Dewar, one of the more legalistic and less imaginative of writers on morality. Dewar, endeavouring to support his thesis that there is a body of natural law, finds himself faced with the same awkward situation as a loyal supporter of "the faith": there is little agreement as to what it is. Dewar bravely tries to minimize his risk. "Even though there be doubt as to what *are* the agreed principles of the Natural Law – and the doubt has been magnified by some writers recently – there is, to say the least, no less doubt as to the exact interpretation of the Sermon on the Mount." To this Fletcher replies: "Exactly so. Both are in the same bad fix."

It is the bad fix in which anyone finds himself who thinks that

110

he has discovered a fool-proof way to the truth, or some method that will ensure it. Even if there are absolutes (a very questionable conclusion) it is obvious that we do not know what they are. Even if new theologians and moralists have discovered ways of working that seem more satisfactory than the old, they are foolish if they think they can guarantee success. To spell out precisely the right and wrong of any situation is as difficult as to spell out the truth and untruth of an argument, which means that it is impossible.

II

Mother Church was at all times a legalist. She maintained that there were revealed laws governing the way God wished us to behave at each moment of our lives. These were laws that could be followed and, though there were some problems about detailing their precise meaning, the general intent was clear. Thus the Ten Commandments set out certain rules that were for all time. To the Ten were added many others, each of which said categorically: "Here is another rule for good conduct; if you keep the rule, you will be good; if you break it, you will be bad."

The evidence for the setting up of tight, never-to-be-broken laws came from two sources: the laws of nature as interpreted by the Church, and the divine law as set down in the Bible, especially in the Old Testament. The natural laws were discovered by examining the normal workings of men and deducing certain rules which were then declared to be universal. The scriptural laws were discovered by analyzing what was written down in the Bible and therefore revealed by God to man. The first process has been followed consistently by the Roman Catholic Church, which quotes the second with approval. The second has been followed consistently by Protestants, chiefly puritans, who do not normally rate the first very high. Both routes, however, lead to the same destination. They are both legalistic.

In practice, it was not possible to maintain the legalistic position ruthlessly. Too many Christians felt compassion for their fellow men, even the heathen, to allow the law to crush everyone all the time, and often even the most undisputed applications proved distasteful. An honest man, driven by the desperation of hunger, would steal a sheep, a loaf of bread, or a small sum of money. The law, never in doubt on such a subject, deriving its authority from rigid theology and its immediate support from bishops and high officials of the established Church, saw clearly what was at stake: the whole fabric of society and morality. Theft was an offence against both natural and divine law. Thus it was decreed; the theft must therefore be punished. Until less than a century ago, the punishment was death. The law was upheld before a general public which could not be trusted to keep its souls unspotted from the world.

Not all the Church felt this way. Certainly not the people, nor the more courageous clergy, nor, to their credit, did many moral theologians. One of the big problems faced by the last group was to reconcile two convictions, both of which they felt strongly, but which were not readily seen as consistent:

1. Here is a clear Law which says that a certain action is *always* wrong.

2. Here is Mr. Smith, who performed the action and, in doing so, really did the right thing.

They resolved the difficulty by the science of casuistry. This word, when it is used at all today, carries overtones of phoney subtlety; and this is understandable. The move from point one to point two, while at the same time keeping the first point intact, led to such intricate mazes of arguments that nobody but a student giving his life to the subject could hope to understand how it all worked out. For, remember, these theologians, driven by their compassion to find some excuse for Mr. Smith, were not allowed to come right out and say that they thought he had done the right thing by breaking the law. They had to show that, in some way, the law had not been truly broken. One is reminded forcibly of those admirable English judges who when faced with absurd precedents in the English Common Law departed from them while putting up a brave front of fulfilling them.

In real life, therefore, there was great uncertainty. The average Christian never knew when he was going to be held responsible by the Church for some law he had broken, or when casuistry was going to come to his rescue. The same uncertainty exists today among Roman Catholics and certain Anglo-Catholics who, believing that there is a natural and divine law that condemns birth control, none the less practise it.

Birth control, in fact, is an excellent example of how change takes place in spite of legalism. Until about fifty years ago, the popular religious idea was that God controlled the birth and death of all his creatures. "When your times comes" is still built into our language as a reminder to us. When God wished you to be born, you were born; when he wished you to die, you died. It was a good theory; it worked. It answered the questions people asked in a world where suffering was a natural hazard. Everything which contained an element of arbitrary cruelty was accepted as "God's will" – he decided.* Therefore, if a married couple, of their own free will, decided to limit the number of children they brought into the world, they were accused of opposing God's will, murdering an unborn child, and defying the laws of nature.

In fact, as we know, and are nowadays willing to pronounce with pleasure, sexual intercourse is the most joyful privilege in the world that can be taken by a man and a woman who wish to become as one person. The act is *in itself* a great and wonderful thing, whether performed inside or outside of marriage. Its wonder and joy, however, is reduced or removed when there is fear. One of the fears which mars such a union is that of having more children than the couple desires; or, especially in a premarital situation, any at all. In order, therefore, to enjoy sexual intercourse to its fullest, which is clearly a good purpose, birth control may be necessary. Yet the law said that to limit the

---

*The week I was writing this, a young woman was delivered of Siamese twins, joined face to face. The father was hopeful. "He is not looking for miracles – but he has a lot of faith in modern medicine." When he first heard the news: "I was numb. When I saw the doctor coming towards me, I knew something was wrong." He felt: "They were just like our other daughter when she was born – except they were joined together. Maybe it was God's will. Maybe he had to have it this way."

number of children born was a sin. It was, as a result, necessary that sexual intercourse be seen as less than a noble relationship in itself and be made justifiable only under certain well-defined and normally joyless regulations.

Alternatively, the process may have taken place another way. Children wère needed. Birth control was wrong. Sexual intercourse was legitimate only when God's will could be worked out in the birth of a child, he alone having the decision to deny such an outcome. In the light of this constant fear, intercourse would inevitably become a less than satisfactory experience, except to those who longed for a child. So there grew up the idea that it is distasteful; that the ideal life is that of virginity; that males, in their weakness, might long to enter women; but that good women, though they receive them (if married to them) dutifully, do not long after it nor actively encourage it.

This negative attitude towards sexual activity was the prevailing one when I was ordained twenty-six years ago. The English prayer book, the only one legal at the time,* came into the open with an honest declaration. "Holy Matrimony is not by any to be enterprized, nor taken in hand unadvisedly, lightly, or wantonly, to satisfy men's carnal lusts and appetites, like brute beasts that have no understanding; but reverently, discreetly, soberly, and in the fear of God." Taken strictly, the words stand up well enough; but the attitude of distaste is all too obvious.

Twenty-six years later, the prayer has changed. Marriage is now "ordained for the hallowing of the union between man and woman; for the procreation of children to be brought up in the fear and nurture of the Lord" (no mention of love, one notices – God is above such Hollywood sloppiness), "and for the mutual society, help, and comfort, that the one ought to have of the other, in both prosperity and adversity."

As the open distaste for sexual activity has declined, there has

---

*The promise I was forced to make, in the presence of the comic-opera paraphernalia of secular and ecclesiastical law was (along with other legal undertakings equally impossible to fulfil) that I would use this book and "none other" except as lawful authority decreed. Lawful authority, following its normal custom, decreed little of value and, though the alternative marriage rite of 1928 was used in some places, it was widely denounced as illegal (which it was) and, in a few cases, court action was threatened.

grown up a new attitude towards birth control. Protestant clergymen in large numbers now attend a gathering organized by a firm which manufactures appropriate medical supplies, and they are delighted. Family Planning is here to stay. It is praised from pulpits, and everyone feels open-minded. Only the officialdom of the Roman Catholic Church, realizing that Protestants have unwittingly knocked down a law and said that it is no longer valid, hold tight. The casuists are at work. It is discovered that certain types of birth control do not break the law; that there are certain times in a woman's life when the law is not broken if devices are used; and, in time, if history is a guide, Catholics will soon be able to practise birth control as freely as Protestants, while at the same time believing it to be against the will of God and the universal natural law.

I have used birth control as an extended example because the issue is decided. Family Planning is now fully respected and respectable. It takes very little imagination to perceive that the same story will be followed through, laboriously and with great suffering on the way, until a similar willingness to accept the approach of situation ethics comes upon people in the areas of pre-marital and extra-marital sexual intercourse, abortions, homosexuality, and so on. It is almost unbelievable today that preachers used to inveigh at great length against masturbation (which they called "self-abuse"). It will one day seem unbelievable that we used to do the same in connection with the other subjects under discussion in this chapter.

III

It is difficult to understand why Mother Church decided to follow after legalism. Jesus Christ spent much of his life denouncing the law. He broke the sabbath. He broke the ritual food laws, saying that they were absurd. He said practically nothing about sexual law; none of the normal puritan shibboleths about sex derive either from Jesus' teaching or his practice. When we turn to St. Paul, we find a still more extraordinary fact: that this great leader, for all his neuroses, did not support legalism at all. He did, of course, accept that there was a law of nature, which even the Gentiles obey. "Although they have no law, they are their own law, for they display the effect of the law inscribed on their hearts." But he goes no further, and his aim in the above passage may not be to establish a universal law of right and wrong so much as to explain that those who do not know the Jewish law have good instincts and can be trusted to find their own morality. He is making what looks suspiciously like a relativistic statement.

That he had in mind something less rigid than a legalistic code can quickly be seen when we look at the rest of his work Over and over, he declares that we cannot be saved by the law. Taken literally, the law is harmful. The most it can do is to bring a destructive consciousness of sin. Only the spirit of the law has any value; its letter is deadly. It does not matter what is lawful so much as what helps the person.

This is not the whole story, of course. St. Paul was a complex character who, in his call for freedom and escape from the tyranny of the law, was still under its thumb. Freed in many respects, he remained a captive in others; himself free, he did not always free other men. Sometimes his argument becomes so entangled that, when he cries, "Does the law then contradict the promises of God?" we half expect him to reply: "Indeed. Haven't I been saying so for the last page?" Instead, caution asserts itself and he answers: "No." He suggests: "The law was a kind of tutor in charge of us until Christ should come, when we should be justified by faith; and now that faith has come, the tutor's charge is at an end." So there it is! We needed to have law (such as the Ten Commandments) until Christ came, when the law would not be needed to control us any more. Why, then, did Christians turn away from what Christ clearly said and pick up the strict law again? Why did Mother Church restore the Ten Commandments which, having been good tutors, were no longer necessary? We may answer at many levels, some of them cynical, but at this moment it is worth noting that Paul himself was aware of the danger. The new freedom from law, he says, is here. "Christ set us free, to be free men. Stand firm, then, and refuse to be tied to the yoke of slavery again."

Paul has more to offer. He is not saying outright that there is no law at all. He is very strong in his attacks on those at Corinth and Ephesus who wiped out the law altogether. Instead, he substitutes a single law: that of love. It is no accident that the most popular chapter with many Christians is I Corinthians 13, in which Paul sums up his whole morality. The key to the nature of man and God is love. Without it, it is useless to have the voice of angels, or of prophecy, to know hidden truths, have great faith, give away everything we own, or become martyrs. Of all things, love is eternal. Everything else will vanish. "There are," he concludes, "three things that last forever: Faith, Hope, and Love; but the greatest of these is Love."

Once identified in the over-all sphere of human existence, he applies it to legalism. Love is the test, and the only test, of moral action. It is the *only* commandment. Jesus had said, "A new commandment give I unto you: that you love one another." This effectively displaced the old ones. The Old Testament itself had foreseen the trend, for the "Summary of the Law,"* the great quotation from the New Testament, is also the great quotation from the Old. The declaration is forthright: the only commandment is that we love. We love God with all our heart, soul, and mind. If the meaning of that eludes us, as it does so many Christians and Jews today, then there is another like it: "You shall love your neighbor as yourself." The one is the other. Paul, obscure though he is when he tangles himself up in abstruse theorizing, comes through with crystal clarity on this. "The whole law," he says, "can be summed up in a single commandment: Love your neighbour as yourself." Just in case we might overlook what he is saying, he goes even further in his letter to the Corinthians:

> Leave no claim outstanding against you, except that of mutual love. *He who loves his neighbour has satisfied every claim of the law.* For the commandments 'Thou shalt not commit adultery, thou shalt not kill, thou shalt not steal,

---

*"The Lord our God is one Lord; and thou shalt love thy God with all thine heart, and with all thy soul, and with all thy might." (Deuteronomy 6:4-5) "Thou shalt love thy neighbour as thyself." (Leviticus 19:18) "Jesus answered, 'The first commandment is, "Hear, O Israel: the Lord your God is the only Lord; love the Lord your God with all your heart, with all your soul, with all your mind, and with all your strength." The second is this: "Love your neighbour as yourself." ' " (Mark 12:29-31)

> thou shalt not covet,' and any other commandment there
> may be, are all summed up in the one rule, 'Love your
> neighbour as yourself.' Love cannot wrong a neighbour;
> therefore the whole law is summed up in love.

We do not, of course, have to agree with Paul; but he is clearly very close to the New Morality, even though he does not apply it well when he takes a look at sex or the family.

What is it, then, that the New Morality says? First of all, it assumes that there are no rules, laws, or regulations to govern moral conduct. Every situation must be judged on its merits, and there is only one test which may legitimately be applied: Is love fulfilled?

The New Moralist does not accept at all the notion that there are moral standards which are revealed by God. He does not believe that God laid down laws which are for all men, at all times, in all nations, under all conditions. He is, therefore, a relativist. He does not accept the "given" in ethics and morals any more than he accepts it in his doctrine or his approach to the Bible. These "given" precepts, including the Ten Commandments, were useful only in those days when they were needed. Since Christ (whether we are Christians or not) we have been freed to be fully ourselves, and there is no more call for sets of precepts. We are free; there is no need to return.

Commandments and moral precepts are not forgotten. They are considered important. But they can only be used as they are tested against love. A man and a woman have committed adultery. The commandment is clearly important. It would be absurd to ignore it, because it was set down by wise men in difficult days, and might still be heard by wise men in difficult days. So we have the commandment before us. Now comes the real test. Is love fulfilled? Not any shallow notion of love, but the real giving of a man to a woman and a woman to a man, the real respect shown for any other people, particularly children, who are involved in the situation and who may be hurt. If love is denied, if there is a mere using of another person for a passing pleasure, if wives and husbands are irreparably hurt, if children are mauled emotionally, then clearly the adultery is not in love. But if love *is* satisfied, then adultery is not wrong. In the case of pre-marital intercourse, the problem is easier. Unlike extra-marital relationships, there is not the same likelihood of damage to innocent people inextricably linked with the situation. That is why those who support the New Morality, while speaking very cautiously about extra-marital relationships, frequently speak in favour of pre-marital ones.

V

Unfortunately, as Paul detected, freedom is not always attractive; the way of Jesus is difficult, and we long to get back to religion, law, obedience, and discipline, all of which are nostalgically recalled. "It reminds us," quotes Fletcher,

> of the Legend of the Grand Inquisitor in Dostoyevsky's novel *The Brothers Karamazov*. It is Ivan's story to Alyosha about the terrible burdens of freedom. Christ returned to earth, and the Spanish Inquisitor, recognizing him in the crowd watching a religious procession, had him arrested at once. In the dead of the night he visited the Christ in secret, embarrassed, trying to explain that most people do not want freedom, they want security. If you really love people, he argued, you make them happy, not free. Freedom is danger, openness. They want law, not responsibility; they want the neurotic comfort of rules, not the spiritual open places of decision-making. They prefer absolutes to relativities. The Christ, he says, must not come back to start again all that old business about freedom and grace and commitment and responsibility. Let things be; just let the Church [the law] handle them. Let him please go away.

The Inquisitor was a man of deep sincerity and, if the Christ were to go away, then the people most relieved would be those who need rules and can see no way to freedom, who are unwilling to receive the responsibility that freedom brings. The fact that by using and playing morality safe there is still no safety cannot be seen because the risk of freedom has not been taken, and there is no desire to take it.

The struggles between the safety-first failures of the legalist and the risk failures of the New Moralist have always been with us; the only difference brought by our modern ways of life is that the legalist can no longer impose his rule upon everyone.

The tension was well brought out by George Bernard Shaw in *Saint Joan*. Joan has appeared before the Grand Inquisitor, dressed in men's clothes, and a charge is laid against her. "She wears," announces d'Estivet, "men's clothes, which is indecent, unnatural, and abominable; and in spite of our most earnest remonstrances and entreaties, she will not change them even to receive the sacrament."

The legalistic approach. There is a rule of morality at stake. To wear men's clothes is immoral. Joan wears men's clothes. Therefore she is immoral. Q.E.D. There is no hole in the syllogism. Grant the first premise and you grant the conclusion. On the way to the inevitable decision, the legalists show their consistency in a delicious piece of dialogue:

> *Inquisitor*: As to the matter of the man's dress. For the last time, will you put off that impudent attire, and dress as becomes your sex?
>
> *Joan*: I will not.
>
> *D'Estivet (pouncing)*: The sin of disobedience, my lord.

Another rule – disobedience to a higher authority – and Joan has broken it. Her reply to the court is essentially a New Morality type of reply. It invokes the assumptions of situation ethics and judges the case, not by the law, but on its merits. "What," she says, "can be plainer commonsense? I was a soldier living among soldiers. I am a prisoner guarded by soldiers. If I were to dress as a woman they would think of me as a woman; and then what would become of me? If I dress as a soldier, they think of me as a soldier, and I can live with them as I do at home with my brothers."

Joan is now in deep trouble. The legalists bring out their last charge. It is familiar to anyone who has urged an acceptance of the New Morality or a new look at the creeds. "You are blinded," says Ladvenu, "by a terrible pride and self-sufficiency." The big trumpet call. Joan is puzzled, as Bishop Robinson must have been when his accusers made the same charge against him. "Why do you say that?" she asks. "I have said nothing wrong. I cannot understand." The Inquisitor has his answer. "The blessed St. Athanasius has laid it down in his creed that those who cannot understand are damned."

Shaw and Dostoyevsky are dealing with the same phenomenon: the struggle between the legalist and the situationist. Shaw dwells on the fact that, in the face of love, the legalist is compassionate and torn apart but has no option. The law must be upheld at all costs. If it appears to conflict with love, then clearly the love is misunderstood. Dostoyevsky deals with the fact that the people like it so; that they need the upholding strength of law and strict morality; that, without it, they collapse into promiscuity and chaos; that they are unable to think responsibly for themselves.

VI

We are faced today with a situation very like that which faced St. Paul. He was brought up under the law as a Pharisee. He came face to face with Christ and knew what it was to be free. He related law to freedom and concluded that there was only one commandment: to love one's neighbour. He did not dismiss the other commandments, they simply took their place as resource pieces, helpful to the person faced with a decision, but only under the one guide-line of love. He did not despise the old law. On the contrary, it was a very wonderful thing, which had helped his ancestors greatly when they needed it most. Thanks to the new freedom in Christ, it was no longer needed. There were no longer rules for all men at all times.

Like Paul, we of the twentieth century have been brought up under the law, especially if we are over forty. It is still assumed in Church rituals, Boy Scout and Girl Guide manuals, day-school ethics, politicians' handouts, and Ann Landers' advice columns that there are clear rules by which we live and that, faced with a difficult decision, we have to apply the rule. To disobey is to fall. The rule is always valid. To this, the New Moralist makes Paul's reply: "We have come face to face with

Christ and know what it is like to be free.* We relate law to freedom and conclude that there is only one guideline: To love one's neighbour." As soon as this is said, we immediately feel the warm winds of a Catholicity which might, indeed, prove universal. We do not dismiss the Commandments. We are not against principles; only against their misuse. So the Commandments, together with all the rest of the natural law and so-called divine revelation, take their place with the remainder of the "given" as resource pieces, to be used when relevant, to be rejected when not; to be considered with great seriousness when they conform to love; to be rejected out of hand immediately they are in conflict with it.

Nor do we despise the old law. On the contrary, it was in many ways a wonderful thing, and helped our grandfathers mightily when they needed it most. It seems a pity that they needed it for so many centuries after the Good News and St. Paul's one Commandment; it seems a still greater pity that so many people need it today. It cannot, however, be despised. There are those who require this type of support, who can operate well only when they are told what is right and wrong, who can decide only when they lay an approved law alongside a situation. Their way of living must be respected. If situation ethics make any sense, freedom must be allowed to those who do not want freedom. They must be allowed their legalism. The new age, however, sets a limit. The freedom to be legalistic stops short of enabling the legalist to impose his philosophy upon those who do not share it.

In other words, the New Moralists may have to assert their own right to freedom. There are many Christians who reject legalism out of hand for themselves, who reject the testing of

* We no longer have to use the word Christ. Because I am an Anglican, I use the word "Christian" frequently. In the words of a laywoman: "I am bugged by Jesus," and I find in him the clearest and fullest declaration of man's freedom to be a man. In our modern pluralist Church, this is only one approach of many. Christ is alive even, to use Robinson's phrase, when he moves among us *incognito*. The classical parable, constantly quoted by New Moralists, is that of the sheep and the goats. Those who were blessed by the judge did not know the Son of Man at all, but helped others in poverty, prison, and hunger. The damned were those who called on him constantly, very religiously, but did not help those in poverty, prison, or hunger.

morals by law, and who must therefore be freed from the legalistic controls which have come to us from a past age and which are
still exercised too widely. How they fight the laws of the country
(which can severely punish doctors who perform a rightful abortion) or the laws of their Church (which can still disdain
pre-marital sexual intercourse) is a matter too vast for a small
chapter in a short book. I am concerned rather with the attitude
of those who accept the ways of working offered by the New
Morality, but who have a nagging fear that this may not be
consistent with their Christian commitment. The hope is that
they will gather confidence. They stand in the tradition of Jesus
Christ and St. Paul, perhaps more than the legalist. There is no
need to feel, as opponents sometimes imply, that the New
Morality is designed to promote Leagues of Promiscuous Bad
Men.

VII

There are many difficulties to be faced. Most of these stem from
the fact, as attackers unwittingly imply, that the standards of the
New Morality are higher than the Old. There are clear limits set
to a law; there are no limits set to love. The standards implied
by the New Morality are, in spite of the constant use of the word
freedom, very severe, because they involve us in responsibility.
The Old Morality involved responsibility at only two points: the
understanding of the law, and its strict application. Realizing
that circumstances often produced injustice, the experts worked
hard at softening the blow, and succeeded. They then went on
to show that the law should still be obeyed and set out every
possible instance in which a Christian might legitimately appear
to disobey while in reality keeping it. Thus, though killing was
specifically forbidden by the law, the casuist allowed you to kill
a man if you were in a war or if he had been convicted of murder.
The believer had to know his law and the sort of circumstances
in which he might – on the surface – act contrary to it. If he did
not know, that was his tough luck. He had resources to help him.
It was not for him to decide; it was for the expert, and he could

find out what the expert thought by approaching his parish priest, either for counselling or through the confessional. It was, therefore, a good system in its day. Now, however, it no longer works. The believer, faced with a decision, is on his own. He is offered one guide-line: love. He is reminded that there are Commandments, and why not look at them first? If he goes for counselling, he will receive it, but it will not be "Thus you must act." He will be asked to find out as much as he can about himself, who he is, what are his relationships with the people he has known, loved, and hated all his life. It is very extensive, and there are no short cuts, no simple knock-down answers. No wonder so many people pine after the good, easy-going old days when somebody else made the decisions.

The higher standards implicit in the New Morality can be seen if we examine the question, raised earlier, of sexual intercourse. Under the Old Morality, the solutions were easy. If you entered a woman, you had to be married to her. Pre-marital and extra-marital intercourse were wrong. This did not prevent such acts from happening, but they were seen to be sins and treated as such. Within marriage, sexual intercourse was considered proper. It was one-sided, the privileges going mostly to the male. If a wife complained, she would be met with some sympathy but would find no support in the law. She was married; her husband had certain privileges known as "conjugal rights," and these could only be taken away for some easily identified medical reason.

Under the one guideline of the New Morality, we can see immediately that the solutions are not simple. Marriage is no longer seen as the test of the rightness or wrongness of sexual relationships. It remains, of course, an overwhelmingly important influence, and will operate against promiscuity as often today as in grandfather's day. Love must be concerned with all the people involved in a situation, all the surrounding circumstances, the possible hurt to others who are loved. The responsibility is indeed so great that if after pondering the commandment to love a couple still engage themselves together, then they may well be justified. Nobody else can judge in general terms; the most we can do (and perhaps this is not possible) is to assess every situation in its own terms. One thing is clear none the less: promiscuity is no more frequent under the New Morality than under the Old, for it is as inconsistent with love as with any other so-called precept. What has happened today is that the test is no longer exclusively that of marriage.

The problems for the New Moralist do not cease here. Under the Old Morality, so long as you kept the law you were safe. The husband could use his wife as he thought fit and feel no pangs of conscience. If a wife died because her husband refused to practise birth control, he would not be charged with immorality. He was married, was he not? In real life, most men were compassionate, and the end result was not very different from that today; yet the law was the ultimate test. The New Moralist, however, has no easy route laid out. Marriage guarantees him nothing of itself. His relationships with his wife are as much under the test of love as his relationships with other women. A woman's relationships with her husband are as much under the test of love as those with other men. A man and a woman, though married, must consider, as carefully as the unmarried, how they belong to one another. If certain conduct is wrong between a man and a woman who are unmarried, it does not become right simply because they are married. Conduct which is right between two married people does not necessarily become wrong because they are unmarried.

VIII

Are there, within the New Morality, any observable standards? This is a legitimate question, to which the answer is "Yes." The difference between the Old Morality and the New is that the former sought the standards out in space, the latter seeks them within the people involved. Perhaps the part of modern life in which this can best be examined is among young people. The young have a reputation with many of their elders for promiscuity and a rejection of all standards. Some, indeed, and rightly, have rejected the standards of their parents; and this is what creates the heated debates which go on. "What is the matter with the young people today?" is a question that comes from the lips of many an Old Moralist. He will then proceed to give statistics of the great increase in juvenile delinquency, illegitimacy, and so on. We must, of course, take a close look at these statistics. They are often emotional, because it is not easy to find statistics for "the good old days." We must set the statistics in context. We have to consider the numbers involved, the types of situation that are being set up for analysis, the type of young person who has been consulted, the part played by the news media in forming impressions, and so on.

I am more concerned, however, with a simple point of attitude. In order to answer the question about young people's moral standards, we have to find out what those standards are. The legalist, discovering that they are not the same as his own, perceives no need for further questions. The New Moralist carries on. If he asks his questions aggressively, he will receive very curt and uncommunicative replies. If he is willing to listen, he will soon find out that young people today have very clear standards, that many live by them and some do not (no new phenomenon among human beings). He will soon find out that the subject matter of this chapter is old hat, left way behind by many of the young people in their search for life.*

What are the standards? They differ from person to person, from group to group; but I can offer my own experience and hope that yours has been the same. They seem to be, above all, compassionate; and they test everything under the guideline of love. I do not find myself greatly at ease with some of their interpretations; I am often embarrassed as their standards are spelled out in conduct. I am, after all, at the age of fifty, a victim of the Old Morality. Yet I have an instinct that the standards of these young people are far higher than those that operated among my own generation. With a fair number of people in my life, and a fair number of situations to assess, I would say that the moral

---

*An example of the more advanced thinking of our young people, which I have found in several groups: "Why, when our chief aim is to help people understand and identify with each other completely, does the Church have such a heavy investment in marriage – an institution which makes such complete sharing between people either enormously difficult or even impossible?"

standards of today are immeasurably beyond those of my day, which were themselves higher than those of my father's day. It may be naïve, but I think that this improvement has come about because, integral to the New Morality, there is a strong element of trust. If you trust people, they normally justify the trust. Identify their own standards and they prove to be better than any that are imposed from outside. What a person discovers in himself is more significant than any standards set out by the cleverest moral theologian who, after all, can do no more than identify his own standards in his own life in the hope that they may be shared by others.

There are no guarantees. In all generations, love has triumphed over law and precept. In all generations, whether the standards are set externally or internally, there are kind people, happily married and unhappily married; there are happy wives and mistresses, whatever the law or absence of it. In all generations, we find both promiscuity and love. The New Morality does not alter this. There were sad tragedies in the old days; there are sad ones today. There has always been emotional violence, and it will not cease.

The New Morality may have done much to improve the moral standards of our day; but this conclusion has no statistics to support it, and there are many, as Larry Solway's "hot-line" radio program bears witness, who take the opposite view. The New Morality has, however, achieved one end which is not disputable. It has freed many people within the Church to say that, though they admire the Ten Commandments (and other law) as resource pieces, they do not feel that they bind all people for all time; and if the authorities insist they must obey the law, they are, given the required circumstances, willing to refuse.

CHAPTER VIII

The New Parish

I

Last year, a group of men and women were drinking coffee before the 11:00 A.M. Sunday Service. They entered a heated discussion and were soon in the middle of a close interchange of personal convictions and beliefs. They had always been friends; they now found themselves in a new relationship with each other. They had not planned it; the meeting was accidental; the new situation was exciting and, for the first time, one at least of the group was seeing another person with clear eyes. A silence fell as a tense moment arrived. It was broken by the ringing of the church bell. One of the group looked at his watch.

"My," he said. "Who'd have thought it? We've been nearly half an hour. We'd better get across to the Church."

One of the others, stung, retorted. "Why should we break up an act of Worship to go and sit in a pew?"

It made sense. The group filled their cups with new coffee and did not break until 1:00 P.M. A single response had wakened them to a consideration of what they had all taken for granted: the parish. What was it? Why was it there? Did it serve any function in the community? What was the point of the old church building? Why did they have to hold services at all? Where did the clergyman fit in? What did it mean to be a parishioner?

Why bother to discuss the parish at all? It is the first question to occur to anyone who has studied the predicament of the modern Church. It is obvious that, in today's world, the parish Church serves a declining purpose. The community in which people live and sleep is important enough; but the community no longer sees the parish Church as serving it. Cars pass each other on the parkways and roads on their way to their respective congregations. The parish system, seen geographically, is in disarray. The parish has become a group of people who assemble in a certain set of buildings and who share a clergyman or staff of clergymen. The work performed is devoted largely to the group who assemble and to such people from outside as they know. The potential is limited.

All this has happened to a generation of churchgoers who feel under an obligation to move to the shops and sidewalks of life rather than the cloisters and altars. It is becoming increasingly evident to any but the blindest of Church members that the important work of the Church takes place in those parts of life which used to be considered peripheral: factories, university campuses, trade unions, financial empires, flophouses, city halls, night clubs, and so on. These are the areas where the action is and where today's decisions are largely made; modern Christians feel that they should be there. Harvey Cox, identifying the challenges that the New Age is making to the New Church, says that the Church can no longer be regarded as the gathered congregation of the parish. Coffee houses, formerly regarded as outposts, are now at the heart of the Church as authentic ministries.

He is right, of course, and more and more churchmen perceive that he is right. Yet his call may have come too late. Enthusiastic as congregations are about the work outside the walls of their Church, it may no longer be possible to fulfil their enthusiasms. For one thing, the authorities devote most of the money and manpower to the parish, which they still see as the heart of the Church, the characteristic task of the priest. A churchwarden in London told me that it was easy enough to squeeze money from

129

the Church Commissioners for material things and for the salaries of clergy; but that it was practically impossible to find any for what he called work among people. A powerful Canadian bishop recently stated that the Parish was, in his opinion, the chief calling for a clergyman. The bishop in question holds the finances of the diocese rigidly in his own hands.

Moreover, as men move into new types of ministry, they are not only denied the necessary support, but are actively embarrassed by an attitude that varies from cool acceptance to scarcely veiled opposition.

Non-parochial ministries are, of course, not new. In the old days, when the parish was considered the only proper sphere for a priest, there were certain jobs outside of it that were considered legitimate and in which some clergy worked with full approval: teaching in a university or private school; acting as a chaplain to a school, university, hospital, or mental institution; writing religious books; becoming an archdeacon or a bishop. None of these professions was directly linked with parish work, but they created few problems, and still create few.

Then there came the worker priests and the industrial chaplains. They had a career far more checkered than the men already listed. For a while they were forbidden to work in France. In London, Colin Cuttell fought hard and gave inspired leadership to the South London Industrial Mission, which is still effective, as is the pioneer work at Sheffield. In Canada, there has been almost nothing, except token chaplaincy work at the ports. In the United States, professional work has been done in New York and San Francisco. For all the high quality of the work achieved, it is pitifully at the edge of official church life. Little is done to ensure that the people engaged have the financial and moral support they need, and most of those who do this crucial work find that they are – in relationship to their colleagues – lonely men.

Throughout the era of the old-style, non-parochial ministries and that of the newer ones, there has existed an anomalous group of clergy at national headquarters. The power of the Church is located at the diocesan level, and diocesan officers include certain clergy who do not work in the parish. Typical are archdeacons concerned with finance and bishops concerned with administration. No questions are raised about the relevance of their work to the Church. Yet, if a clergyman undertakes the same style of work at national headquarters, whether in London, New York, or Toronto, his ministry is perceived, to some extent, as irregular. Certainly different arrangements have to be made in order, as the chancellor of my own diocese tactfully and yet significantly expressed it, to "regularize the ministry."

More recently, clergy have been entering the fields of counselling, social work, public education, insurance, and so on. If they are employed and paid exclusively by secular agencies, there are some consequent problems. The priest thinks that his employment is more appropriate to the modern ministry than work in a parish, and that his vocation is best fulfilled in this way. Yet, when he does so, he is asked to explain himself in ways never demanded, for example, of a chaplain to a snob school. It is sometimes implied that he is "leaving the ministry," and many men who have taken this step feel that they are treated by their bishops as second-class Church citizens. Many clergy are now entering these new ministries; more will do so in the future. Yet the institutional Church still finds difficulty in recognizing them, not only as legitimate but, if Cox is correct, more at the heart of the modern Church than the parish. For, when they enter secular employment, they do so in the same way as any other employee. Their function is to do a good job. It is here, because there are no clearly perceived "spiritual" tasks, that the officialdom of the Church feels the pinch. Perhaps this last group is not too important. The men involved will survive and, because the official Church does not pay their salaries, it cannot ultimately deprive the work of its vitality.

There remain, however, the parish and such non-parochial work as is paid for directly by the Church. Is there any hope of change? There are, it seems to me, two principal ways in which the Church can respond to the situation in which it finds itself. The first will be disastrous, but is a real threat. The second, using the parish, will provide an indirect road to a new way of working in the world.

The first response would be a battening down of the hatches, an attempt to preserve at all costs what little remains of past glories. It would take the form of giving powerful support to those segments of the Church that oppose change and strive to maintain the *status quo*. This would have the effect of stifling new, experimental work because most of the money can be supplied from only one source: the parish. It is a strange irony that the parish is the only source of income for work that takes place outside itself and may eventually destroy it. It is, therefore, in the parish that fears can most quickly be aroused and entrenchment can most readily be encouraged.

In the days of its great power and wealth, the Church might easily have provided the resources for both the continuance of the normal parish structure and also the development of new ministries outside. Instead, congregations invested heavily in buildings too large for practical use; in huge organs; in parish halls designed for annual functions; and in masses of expensive fittings. These now constitute the unrealizable wealth of the diocese of Toronto in which I live, of most English dioceses, and of many American ones as well.*

At this moment, with wealth that cannot be converted into money, and congregational donations (in terms of real money) shrinking, the Church has to decide what to do. The shrinking will not end. Without analyzing why people supported their other business firm, must decide what it will keep and what it Church years ago, the fact is that they feel little need to do so today. In a situation of declining income, the Church, like any will cut.

If the Church follows the destructive path of self-maintenance at all costs – and events do not encourage excessive optimism – it

---

*The Americans came out of the wealthy era more successfully than either the English or the Canadians. They were able to set up their "peripheral" ministries when it was possible to finance them, and they are now established. The English also, perhaps due to the fortuitous possession of strangely worded endowments and trust funds, were able to set up creative non-parochial work. Canadian efforts have been trivial and amateurish by comparison, because the nation is only now coming alive and, as it does so, finding that it does not need the Church.

will clearly cut out those ministries that are considered unimportant. Women first, of course, because the Church has always despised women, paid them starvation wages, and made no attempt to treat them honourably. Women are expendable. They will be asked to work under shameful conditions in return for a mere pittance. (Some women workers, with good reason, may think that this has always been the case.) Then there will have to go those ministries that do not supply money to the institution and which, in fact, cost money. These are the ministries outside the parish. Bishops and archdeacons will be retained; those that appeal to the charitable instincts of worshippers will survive. But the rest – including chaplaincy work of an original style, all research work, and staff work at national headquarters* – will find themselves without adequate funds. The prime aim will be to ensure that provision is made for diocesan and parish clergy, together with such necessary staff as organists.

The palmy days are over. Brave people strive to lead congregations into what is euphemistically termed "stewardship," but they cannot turn back the tide. Incomes decline and, if dioceses decide to cut down their support for outside work, who can blame them? It is the duty of every man to protect his own.

It will not work, of course. Once a disastrous decision is made to hang on at all costs, then the next stage quickly comes. Already we can see what has happened in Europe; it will happen on the American continent. There will, however, be some difference in the observable effects. Not possessing the endowments of the Church of England, the Canadian Church will eventually have to close some parishes. The process will be conducted with the minimum of embarrassment to the declining congregations; but it will be done until the Church consists of those parishes that can afford to maintain themselves, plus the downtown Churches needed to supply some answer to the consciences of those who feel that more is involved in life than self-preservation. The parish will then appear to the general public in the same guise as a monastery does today: admirable and exotically attractive, but not especially relevant.

---

*This has already begun. The money available is being drastically reduced to a point where professional work is becoming almost impossible.

IV

There is, however, another possible way of responding to today's predicament, and there are some signs that this will be the Church's way into the future. More and more members of our congregations realize that the institutional Church is in decay; they know that the parish is no longer filling an appreciated need; yet they are not willing to shrug it off. What are they to do? They know that the important work of the Church lies outside the parish, and yet it is in the parish that they can most naturally work at the moment. It is here, to say the least, that any money must be found. If there is to be any reaching out to the secular life, the Christian will likely find the start of it in his parish.

That is why the remark quoted at the beginning of this chapter is important. Why should members of a congregation break up an act of worship over coffee in order to sit in a pew, which may prove a waste of time? Jesus was "the man for others"; the parishioners of the modern parish must become men for others. To do so, they must know themselves. They do not have to give up the parish; but they have to reconstruct it.

The first step is to recognize the fundamental purpose of the parish: to provide a situation in which people can meet together. It is impossible for a person to find himself by himself. He needs company. He needs to share his convictions, his hopes, his fears, his miseries, his hatreds, his loves. He can do this anywhere; but, in present-day society, the parish may still be his best gamble. It is established in every part of the country; it is available. Wherever he goes, whatever his job, whatever his background, he can find a building, to say the least, where people assemble. At the moment, most of these groups are authoritarian. This need not be so; and it is offering the simplest of targets to suggest that it can quickly end, once the principle is grasped that a parish is a meeting place.

Having met, what does the congregation do? Facing the pluralism of our modern society, and accepting it joyfully, members meet for any purpose they think worth while. Notice: which *they* think worthwhile – not the bishop, the synod, or the archdeacon; not the canons or the prayer book.

Different people have different aims and personalities. It is not difficult, however, to imagine the types of people who will be meeting together. Here are a few:

1. There will be those who wish to know themselves deeply. They will engage in groups that meet without an agenda and simply discuss and share whatever comes into their minds. They will find themselves. If people talk long enough, they begin to speak the truth. If the agreed principle is honesty of sharing, they will soon achieve it or will leave the group. In such situations, there is always discovery. Some of it is hurtful; none of it is harmful. We come to know ourselves and we soon know others. Whereas we have usually thought that our problems were unique, that we were the only people with such anger and guilt, with such overwhelming hostility and love, we find that everyone is cast in a similar mould, though no two are the same. We all love and hate. A group that meets regularly simply to talk about its members inevitably discovers this. One of the big complaints made by opponents is that the free-wheeling group, with no agenda and no agreed educational content, simply shares the members' common ignorance. This is untrue. They share their love and their hate. Besides this, little else matters.

2. There will be those who do not wish to face themselves in this way. If they try such a group as the previous one, they will, if they are wise, quickly leave it. It is not for everybody to dig deeply into himself and others. So they will find some group that can share their desires. Perhaps they want to know about some things. Why not find out? It may be the Bible. It may be Harvey Cox's *The Secular City*. It may be William Temple or Charles Gore. There is no limit set. Such groups, assembled to discuss a topic, often finish up considering themselves; but this is natural.

3. In the modern world, we have an untold wealth of aid in considering the normal and abnormal behaviour of human beings. In particular, there is the sensitive work done by psychologists, psychiatrists, social workers, and so on. These are rarely "Christian" in the old-fashioned sense of the word; but they are usually Christian in the sense presumed in Chapter III and

135

Chapter IV of this book. In other words, faced with a request to help others, they will help. Some refuse but, so long as they are not asked to accept some creed, many accept. A group in a parish may, therefore, freely invite into their midst professionally trained experts who can help them. In this way, they may without difficulty set up therapy groups. Of these there are many types: art-therapy groups, psycho-drama groups, and even groups in which individual therapy may prove possible. There is clearly some expense, because the psychiatrist or other professional ought to be paid; but this should cost no more than our present pipe organs, stained-glass windows, and once-a-week gothic buildings. And we would be dealing with people, not things.

4. There are, especially in parishes near or in the heart of cities, always problems that call for immediate help. There are bums, outcasts, and misfits. Some people, ill at ease with therapy groups or free-discussion groups, unanxious to learn the facts about anything, long to give water to the thirsty, food to the hungry, shelter to those without it, and freedom to the prisoner. The parish can provide them with the chance to do this. Many already do, especially those that understand housing problems, inadequate social services, poor medical services, and so on. If the Church shows itself to possess members whose heart is given to helping others, it is here that it shows itself most clearly. It is one of the minor tragedies of those parishes that work so success-fully that there is sometimes a vocal group of "respectable" people who resent devoting time to bums, prostitutes, and homosexuals that should, they imply, be given to more godly enterprises, like Bible study and prayer groups.

5. Not that prayer groups and Bible-study groups are to be set aside. They come, however, under my second heading as groups with specific study projects and are not to be regarded as different. A serious mistake is made if it is assumed that study of a Bible passage is better than a study of Bernard Shaw; that a prayer meeting is better than a therapy group. In other words, there are certain traditional activities that the Church must dis-cover simply as expressions of the particular desire of the people involved. There are those who enjoy decorating, and why not?

Let them be members of altar guilds, sewing groups, and so on. They are not to be thought of, in any way, as second-class citizens of the Church. Nor, on the other hand, may they think of themselves as somehow closer to God or the Church because they are concerned with altars and Sunday Services. A coloured picture of King David or Jesus remains simply a piece of colouring, no more religious or useful than colouring Donald Duck. Similarly, to deck out an altar with linen, flowers, and brass is neither more nor less godly than to set up a coffee house. In the present-day parish, the second may legitimately be preferred; but there is no fundamental difference. To sing hymns and anthems is an exercise which brings people together in a common activity. Its chief value is that they sing together. Of equal value is singing together in a performance of *Oklahoma* or a concert put on by young people with guitars. A pageant about the Church, or a nativity play, is neither more nor less relevant than *The Night of the Iguana*. The Psalms are great; so are the latest folk songs.

V

So far, I have described certain types of group which people might join, making provision for a wide variety of temperament. There are many other groups, and I only offer the above as representative. One element, however, is crucial. The purpose of a group is in terms of love, not of duty. The modern parish accepts that there is no need to perpetuate an organization, *whatever it is*. It does not concern itself with membership lists, growths, or declines. Groups of people last as long as they last; perhaps for a couple of meetings, perhaps for years. Nobody need worry if a group decides to disband. Why not? There need be no speeches of lament, no exhortations to please join. If people are interested, they provide their own resources; it is as simple as that. The anxious plea from the group scoutmaster is not necessary. If scouting brings boys together in a way which fathers appreciate, there is no need for appeals. If the help, due to carelessness or ignorance of the need, is not forthcoming, it may be mentioned and, if there is no response, the troop may well close down. There is no loss. If the need is great, the closure will soon be reversed, and the fathers will be helping. If their enthusiasm wanes, then close again. If the boys are keen, they will find ways of staying together. If they are not, what is the point of forcing the matter?'

One of the saddest inflictions imposed on members of an organization by other members is the terrible fear of failure; the thought that, if a movement comes to an end, the existing members are to blame. It is a fear that besets the Church. Perhaps due to a lingering sense of infallibility, perhaps to the delusion that God prefers church activities to night clubs, nobody can accept failure effortlessly. Somehow it seems like an insult to God. We make an impassioned plea for the guidance of the Holy Spirit, and the ensuing meeting is a shambles. To admit the failure sounds like a denial of the Holy Spirit as well as ourselves. Yet today there need be no fear of admitting failure, because there are no facts, beliefs, or practices that have to be imposed from "out there." There is nothing awful about a club closing down. There is no need to feel desolate when a church closes down. If people want it, it will survive. If they do not, why should the tears flow beyond the normal human regret at seeing something, once valued, disappear?

The strange irony is that, in parishes like the one I am describing,* there is less willingness to disband than in those parishes that are anxious to maintain themselves at all costs. Perceiving that the rector is not willing to turn up to all their meetings, not willing to take them off any hooks, not willing to make pretence that all is running well, and – above all – not going to question the way they do things or the standards they adopt, the people involved become fully responsible. They are on their own. They must discover their own principles and standards of operation; and this they do.

---

*Though this chapter commits nobody else to the opinions expressed in it, the work described is largely that of Holy Trinity in Toronto (as seen through my eyes). The Rector is the prophetic and vibrant James Fisk; the activities outlined here prove to be highly practicable.

VI

The portrait so far is still one of small groups. Do these groups ever meet each other? Is there any way in which they can assemble in common? In simple terms, the answer to this is the Church Service. This becomes very evident whenever large numbers of people meet, even in a parish that is endeavouring to respond to the modern world in the way outlined here. A vestry meeting is called to discuss the future ministry of the parish, and everyone clearly understands that this means *their* ministry, not the rector's under their instruction. The meeting concentrates on the various work undertaken by different groups within the congregation. The work is exciting; but the meeting is not exciting. Individual people suddenly become involved in an issue, interest is expressed, help offered. There is little controversy, because the tasks are what they want them to be. Then, when it seems as if all that is required is to identify some new areas of work, a member stands up and asks: "How far to the Left is our Church going to go?" Everyone knows what the words mean, though their interpretations may be different from that of the speaker. It is the Sunday Service that is being referred to. Are there, asks the speaker, certain beliefs – perhaps in the creed – that Anglicans have to accept? The meeting is in a hubbub. Something has been said that scratches everyone. It is immediately obvious that most members present have something to say, and that many are highly personal reactions. That there are two main groups is quickly evident. There are those who resent the changes which have been going on, and hanker for the Service as they recall it from the past. There are those who want exploration and experiment. They have come to this Church for that very reason. They say that they have left their other parishes because the Services were dull and meaningless; and they would not wish to see any return.

All this is said at once, and little clear meaning may be gathered. The leader suggests that the meeting break into small groups to discuss what questions they would like to raise. This they do, and the matter rests. An important discovery has been made. Even in a parish, which is ready to change, even among people who welcome change and wish it to become more challenging and exploratory, the Service *matters*.

Furthermore, those who stand outside the Church agree. They are willing, sometimes eager, to share in the activity of the smaller groups; but they do not wish to attend the common worship. They recognize it, however, as a legitimate and typical activity of the parish. They approve of it – for others. If the Worship is something they can understand, and does not demand that they think like mediaeval monks, they may even share in it from time to time. Even if they never share, they recognize, along with the ones who do, that there is a need to assemble in some activity which can be seen as the worship of the whole congregation.

But how?

It is obvious that our present Services are useless. By this, I do not mean that they are useless for all people, or that those who have a great investment in them are short in intelligence. I mean simply that they can no longer be the means by which a whole congregation can share something which they recognise as important to their whole life. Some can, of course. Prayer-book services, Holy Communion and Morning Prayer, set intercescessions, anthems, hymns, standardized sermons, pews, choirs, vestments, organs, altars, sanctuaries: all these appeal to enough people to be considered a legitimate and important part of parish activity. It may be expected and hoped that just as some people find themselves in a painting group, so others find themselves in a traditional ceremony known as Holy Communion. It will, for a long time to come, be a larger group than the former, though the signs are that this will not last forever.

The conduct of prayer-book services then becomes one important activity, and no more, of the modern parish. Those who wish to go, go. If enthusiasm wanes and attendance drops too low then, as with any other activity, there is no need to despair. Close down Morning Service as cheerfully as you would let the men's club close down. There is no need to feel a sense of failure; much less need to feel guilty. There is no more reason for people to go to Church than to any other meeting.

VII

We are still, however, left with the congregation's desire to meet together. Here much care is required, much compromise. The meetings will not be able to follow the same pattern each time. Perhaps, in the early stages, a meal is the best assembly. It brings people together on common ground. Everyone likes to eat, and a meal provides a shared atmosphere of belonging to each other. There are strong links with the Last Supper, as the sharing of food becomes an important sacrament for those who eat it. At a later stage, once it is clearly seen why the people are coming together, then different ways of holding the common meeting may be devised. Some of these different ways will include a return to more ancient methods. It is likely, for example, that the coming together at such times as Christmas and Easter may take the form of a High Mass, conducted with the full panoply of mediaeval-style joyfulness. Nothing has been said in this chapter that excludes previous methods; the whole plea is that the joys and truths which have come to us from the past take their place alongside our new ones as equals. There is no desire to urge that all that is past is dead any more than that all that is past is alive.

Difficulties remain. People vary much, and it is impossible to meet everyone's needs at once. Some want children to be dancing around during their assembly, blowing on toy instruments, banging drums. Others find children irritating, no matter how much they love them and try to close their ears. Some children are at home in large groups; others are shy and frightened. These are simple facts. It is obvious, then, that our assembly may quickly have to divide if it is held very often. And why not? There is no way in which the *whole* Church can ever meet together. We have learned to accept the fact that a congregation of several hundred worshipping in a large Church somehow represents the whole. There is no reason why a hundred should not achieve the same, or fifty, or ten, or two or three gathered together. There is no merit in size. A large congregation has no more intrinsic meaning than a small one. Therefore, if the assembly is held, say, weekly, then there may have to be more than one meeting. This, on the surface, looks perhaps the most attractive because it is the nearest to our present way. Already there are many parishes that scarcely use the prayer book at an early service and follow it closely at the eleven o'clock service.

There is another approach, however. Why must the assembly be weekly? There is nothing wonderful about Sunday. We are now freed from the assumption that it differs from any other day of the week. In the past, it was necessary to protect some leisure for the masses of the people. The American Indian knew nothing of a sabbath, and the tribes suffered indescribably as a result. In days when we have a five-day week, with a four-day week round the corner, there is nothing to fear. Leisure is guaranteed.

Jesus gave us the clue. "The sabbath," he said, "was made for man." As soon as man no longer needs it, it can be set aside. The early Christians made a small change, from Saturday to Sunday. The past century has taken the misery out of Sunday, so that very few people treat is as wholly different from the rest of the week. Now we can complete the process. We do not need a day of leisure because there is no danger of losing our spare time; we do not need it for our common assembly, which can take place any day. The better the deed, the better the day.

Just as the assembly may take place on any day of the week, so it may take place, not only as often as we please, but as rarely. If it seemed best, the common-worship assembly might take place perhaps only three times a year, perhaps only annually. Frequency is synonymous only with frequency.

VIII

What is to happen at the assembly? In the liturgical discoveries of the past fifty years, it was soon detected that worship must be a celebration. It must celebrate the normal activities of man in his normal life. The worship assembly had, in some way, to be one in which people came to know each other. The first steps, still popular, took the form of adapting dull rituals and cere-monials to bright ones. It worked very well. Jazz masses were written; people danced the mass; congregations danced in Church at Easter time to "Lord of the Dance"; there was an immediacy about the music and the singing in general. New prayers were written in English instead of near-Latin. The Service showed signs of becoming popular. The surge of enthusiasm is still strong, especially among young people. It shows that they want life where they felt there had been death. Unfortunately, the most that could be hoped for from this particular type of experiment was to make vivid and enthusiastic an activity that could never become the common assembly. The worshippers still assembled to worship a God *out there*. The creed, sung to Geoffrey Beaumont, might seem more alive than the creed sung to Merbecke; and the "Missa Luba" is a triumphant happiness. But it is still the creed. The peripheral formulae may change as much as you please but, if the deep elements remains the same, then not enough change has taken place. That is why, though Roman Catholic, United, Methodist, and Anglican Services vary enormously, each Church has members who find them dull. As Ernest Howse pointed out, our Churches are dividing horizontally, and we may be due for a new style of alignment. In every Church, there are those who say: "You know, the Roman Catholics (or the Protestants) are really Christian when you get right down to it; but I don't know that I trust that coffee-house gang in our own Church."

Such outward changes, as I have implied, should be warmly encouraged. But, if we are realistic, our hopes should not extend any further than that one segment of a parish will attend a traditional type of worship in a more modern style.

IX

These are some of the directions in which the parish may move, unless it elects to die slowly in the fashion described at the beginning of this chapter. Even such directions will not ensure life beyond the needs and work of the congregations. Yet it is in the parish, in its groups, that people will probably find those common elements that enable them to be free in themselves and free with others. At the moment, it is difficult to imagine any other assembly or group doing this, or allowing it to be done easily.

In all this, the parish recognizes that, in modern society, it is simply one section of the population. It recognizes gladly that there are other groups at work, that there are other ways of achieving our full maturity, that there are other methods of operating. A parish is justified by what it is within these limits. To know some other people deeply – this is a purpose that the new parish may hope to fulfil. Anything more, such as the desire to convert the whole world, is unreal to the believer and claptrap to the unconvinced onlooker.

When one examines the possible future of parishes of this type, it is apparent that few of the functions described clearly fall within the present style of clergymen. There will be need for a staff, and the staff will call for someone who, no matter in how democratic a fashion, will be seen as the principal. This does not require ordination in the traditional sense. There is no reason why a layman should any longer be excluded from celebrating the Holy Communion. And this includes women – for the old distinctions, never justified, are now completely inappropriate.

We already have an example of what might happen if our present style of ministry comes to an end; and, fortunately, it shows that no catastrophe is likely to result. If we go back a century, we shall find that the head people in universities were always clergymen. They were often called rectors. Nowadays these head people are mostly laymen. The educational standards of the institutions of which they are principals, far from declining, have moved ahead. There is good reason to think that lay rectors of parishes would prove as effective. There will, as with universities, necessarily be an interim period; for there are still many clerical rectors who must be fed, clothed, and housed in recognition, not only of their vocations, but also of the fact that so many of them are highly efficient. None the less, in the doing of their work, they will begin to behave more like laymen. This is perhaps one of the brightest hopes of those who wish the parish to survive.

Once a parish has been established on these lines, then there ought to be little difficulty about solving the problem of how much work is to be internal and how much external. It will be a parish in and of the world, and everything it does will be part of the world. The words "inside" and "outside" will cease to have much significance. There will be realization that there is no longer any area of life that is especially holy. Everything is holy; or, if you prefer, nothing is holy.

X

One problem remains. There are those who find it impossible to accept that Church attendance is but one part of a parish's activity, neither more nor less than any other. They feel that services, Bible-reading, prayer, and similar activities head a list of priorities, and that this list is not simply one that happens to suit them; it is one that every Christian should accept. Such a list appears in the present Anglican prayer book. As in doctrine and ethics, these people are legalistic in their approach to worship. There is a right way to worship God, and he has revealed what it is. There is no obvious manner in which such people may become happy in the new parish, so long as they feel that God prefers certain activities, that an empty Church means an empty parish life, and that God must weep at dusty altars. The dissonance involved for many of these people would be too great. At the moment, of course, more than ample provision is made for them; in fact, the problems lie at the other end of the spectrum – namely, that those parishes that are exploring *new* ways of ministry are constantly being censured. This may prove temporary, however. Twenty years hence, perhaps less, the majority of parishes will either have vanished, retreated into a shell, or be in the new pattern. It is when we reach this stage that great care will have to be taken to make sure that those who have strict legalistic opinions and beliefs will be fully accepted. Separation is lamentable, but it may prove impossible to assemble together those who see traditional doctrine, ethics, and worship as one way among many and those who see them as one truth. If, by some miracle, they can be assembled together without intolerable distortion, then the peak of rejoicing will be reached.

XI

This book will conclude with some practical help. In the parish of Holy Trinity, Toronto, a Religious Education Committee has been at work for a long time trying to decide how best to help the congregation discover its purpose. The Committee produced a short report which is being circulated among the congregation and will be discussed at length during the fall and winter of 1966-67. The report expresses the differences that exist on the Committee itself; but this is of no moment. The purpose of the document, written by Catherine Gallup, is to help the members of the congregation think about themselves and come to some conclusions, no matter how provisional those conclusions may be.

What the results will be cannot be foretold, and this is a good thing. The report is offered here on the chance that it may appeal to other groups which are concerned about their common life, that they might find it useful to study in their parishes or whatever the context of their meeting together. Here it is, in a slightly shortened form.

During the past year, the Christian Education Committee has been considering what the purpose and function of Holy Trinity should be. In considering this, two points emerged which have led us to put forward a proposal for the reorganisation of the life of the congregation. The two points are:

I   *A wide diversity of beliefs* among the members of the committee, which reflects the diversity of beliefs in the congregation as a whole. For some members, traditional forms of worship provide an essential source of strength by which they carry on their daily work; for others, they have become meaningless. Some find the concept of God almost without meaning; others can subscribe to every clause of the creed. Amid all this divergence, the Committee found that they agreed on three things:

1. That the life of Jesus provides a focus for their lives.
2. That they value very highly the fellowship they have with other members of the congregation, whether they agree together or not.
3. That the congregation must be outward-looking as well as inward-looking.

II   *The inadequacy of the present organisation,* in which the responsibility lies with the rector and churchwardens, while the rest of the congregation are denied their share of responsibility. This situation bears little resemblance to St. Paul's picture of the Church in I Corinthians 12, where he compares it to a body in which each organ has its own particular function and each is essential to the well-being of the body.

With these two points in mind, the Committee has tried to draw up a plan for the life of the congregation so that there can be room within it for people of widely different beliefs and so that as many members of the congregation as are willing to do so may share in the responsibility for its life, and be able to regard themselves as ministers with their own particular ministry to perform.

Proposed Plan for Holy Trinity Congregation

1. The congregation is a fellowship of people committed to one another who, through their life together and its focus on the life of Jesus, are striving to grow in love and in the discovery of the fullness of their humanity. When this growth is taking place, it will find expression in concern for the needs of people outside the congregation.
2. Within the life of this fellowship a wide diversity of ways is provided for people to grow through their life together. Groups are set up to engage in a particular activity, e.g., Bible study, traditional forms of worship, art, study of a particular book or topic, Anglican Church women, psycho-drama, concern with policy for Friendship Centre, plays, and stories, etc. Members of

these groups commit themselves to attendance of their group for a period of four months (September to December; January to April). Most of these groups are small (six to ten people). All these groups must be approved by the whole fellowship so that an underlying unity of purpose may be maintained.

3. The fellowship expresses its concern for people outside in about five different areas of operation: work among deprived people; the restaurant and coffee house; the Social Service Centre; the business community; and municipal government. These concerns have to be adopted and approved by the whole fellowship.

4. The whole fellowship meets together on Sunday morning to discuss the various activities and to break bread together. This breaking of bread is a symbolic meal expressing the fellowship's desire for unity and common life and purpose. The similarity between this meal and the Last Supper is obvious, but it should not be called Eucharist or Communion. These last words will continue to represent the traditional forms of service which will be taking place at other times.

5. All meetings of the fellowship may be attended by anyone.

6. All members who are willing to share in responsibility for the life of the fellowship and to regard themselves as having a particular function to perform may become ministers.

7. All ministers make a definite commitment which is undertaken on a yearly basis. This commitment involves:

(a) The giving of money.
(b) Belonging to one of the groups listed under 2 above.
(c) Giving of service either within the life of the fellowship or in one of the five areas of concern listed under 3 above.

8. The ministers elect annually a committee of ten (including representatives from each of the five areas of concern) to be the governing body of the fellowship.

9. Paid officers of the fellowship are: a treasurer, a caretaker, and a secretary-administrator who will keep in touch with members and co-ordinate their activities.

148

10. Many of the activities of the fellowship will require a leader appointed for a particular function: presiding at the Sunday meetings; leading the various types of small groups; performing marriage and funeral rites; counselling members of the fellowship and helping them discover their own ministry in terms of the commitments listed under 7 above. Ordained clergy may be needed for a few of these functions, but most of them may be performed by lay people. It may not be necessary to have any full-time ordained clergy.

11. Children may attend the Sunday morning meetings. Experience in working in small groups is provided for those old enough to benefit. Children are eligible to become ministers when they are capable of making the three commitments listed under 7 above .

It is obvious that the above document is unlikely to receive the unanimous approval of the congregation, and there would be cause for alarm if it did. It does, however, set out clearly some of the practical consequences for the Church, if even a proportion of the ideas described in this book is well based. Should the Church survive at all, it will be one in which fixed creedal doctrines, set liturgies, and authoritarian ethical standards will play little part. It will be concerned with people and the way of the community at large. If it sets out to judge at all, it will judge every situation on its merits. When compared with the present Church, it will be scarcely recognizable, and some readers may feel that the word "Church" is inappropriate. Yet when we compare the Church of the past with that of today, we find that the differences are as great, perhaps greater, than between the present Church and that of the future as perceived here. If we have journeyed from the past to a vastly different present, it is surely reasonable to suppose that we may journey from the present to a vastly different future. Life is change and a Church which does not evolve will die.

RENEWALS 458-4574